FROM THE AIR
Britain's Railways
THEN & NOW

FROM THE AIR
Britain's Railways
THEN & NOW

Aerofilms

Ian Allan
PUBLISHING

INTRODUCTION

The success of *Britain's Railways from the Air Then & Now* indicated that there was considerable interest in the unique perspective that aerial photography gives to the study of railways in the landscape and of changes to that landscape over a period of time.

The first volume incorporated a small fraction of the archive available from Aerofilms and the scale of the company's collection is such that it is possible to produce a further selection. The first volume covered, to a large extent, many of the major towns and cities of the United Kingdom along with many of the traditional railway towns. With this new selection, although a number of the country's major cities have been revisited, the opportunity has been taken to explore to a significant extent the interrelationship between the railways and the traditional heavy industries— coal, iron and shipbuilding—and how the decline in one has been mirrored by the decimation of the other.

As with the previous volume, there are a number of self-evident elements that become immediately apparent when recording railways from the air. The first of these is the sheer scale of the railway infrastructure until comparatively recent times; the decline in facilities, particularly in freight terms, over the past 30 or 40 years is quite frightening. The second element that becomes all too apparent, is the scale to which many towns and cities have grown over the past 40 years. The concept of 'urban sprawl' is well recognised; it is only through aerial photography that the actuality becomes clear. The idea of a 'green and pleasant land' is becoming a fiction for much of the United Kingdom.

It should be noted that, whilst every effort has been made to replicate as far as possible, the camera angles from the earlier photographs, for a number of reasons— such as suitable flight paths in Britain's ever more congested air space, weather and differing types of camera—this has not always proved completely possible. The angles selected, however, do allow for a detailed comparison between the historic scenes and those of the present day. It should also be noted that all the contemporary photography was specifically undertaken by Aerofilms for this book.

LEEDS

Then: 17 April 1952
Now: 24 January 2001

Although Leeds' traditional industries may have declined, the city has carved itself a second career as one of the country's major regional financial centres over recent years and, as a result, it has tasted unexpected growth and prosperity — growth and prosperity that has resulted in the rebuilt station of the 1960s now proving to be inadequate. At the time the 'Now' photograph was taken, Leeds City station was starting to return to a degree of normality following a period of temporary closure in part as a result of remodelling the section from the station westwards in an endeavour to increase track capacity to serve the newly enlarged station. The temporary cessation of services had not been without its problems, but the improvement resulting from the upgrade should facilitate ease of operation in the future.

The first of these photographs shows the scale of station in the early 1950s. Although called Leeds City since 2 May 1938, the station itself, as shown in this photograph, was composed of two distinct sections. To the north was Leeds Wellington, the ex-Midland Railway station, whilst to the south (and provided with the through platforms heading eastwards to Selby) was Leeds New, which was jointly controlled by the North Eastern and London & North Western railways. Wellington station initially opened on 1 July 1846 and the temporary station then provided was rebuilt in 1850. The MR-owned Queens Hotel was originally constructed in the early 1860s, but the structure illustrated here was the result of a complete reconstruction, to the design of Curtis Green and William Hamlyn, that was reopened on 12 November 1937. The concourse area of Wellington station was rebuilt at the same time. Leeds New station was opened on 1 April 1869 and was enlarged as from 5 January 1879.

In 1963 the decision was taken to centralise all of Leeds' passenger services on a rebuilt Leeds City station on the site of the existing New station. When the modernisation was complete, passenger facilities were withdrawn from the city's other station, Central (Wellington had lost its passenger services on 13 June 1966 when it was converted into a parcels depot), and the approaches from the west, through Whitehall Junction, were modified. Initial expectations — given the fact that it was widely believed that services to Ilkley and through the Aire Valley would not survive — was that the modified four-track layout would suffice. However, the planned closures did not occur and this, compounded by the fact that the alternative route into the city from Wakefield was disconnected as part of the electrification of the East Coast main line and by rapidly expanding traffic on the suburban routes, ensured that track capacity on the western approaches to Leeds was insufficient. In the late 1990s, Railtrack took the decision to modify these approaches by adding two extra running lines and also to increase the platform capacity at Leeds City station.

The 'Now' photograph records the scene at Leeds City in late January 2001, during the construction period. Over the Christmas/New Year period, much of Leeds City was inaccessible and, much to the annoyance of both operators and passengers, the engineering occupation had lasted longer than planned. Indeed, when the photograph was taken, services were still being disrupted and clear evidence of the occupation can be seen in the presence of several engineering vehicles in the station. Clearly visible is the new roofing constructed over the southern part of the station (over new platforms 16 and 17) and on the north (over rebuilt platforms 1 to 5). Note also the new footbridge constructed at the west end of the 1967 overall roof. It is expected that work will be completed by the autumn of 2001, when platform 17 will be commissioned. **(A42477C/687565)**

CONTENTS

First published 2001

ISBN 0 7110 2729 3

© (Photography) Aerofilms Ltd 2001
© (Text) Ian Allan Publishing Ltd 2001

Published by Ian Allan Publishing

an imprint of Ian Allan Publishing Ltd, Hersham, Surrey KT12 4RG; and printed by Ian Allan Printing Ltd, Hersham, Surrey KT12 4RG.

Code: 0106/A2

ABERDEEN

Then: 18 October 1938
Now: 12 January 2001

The 'Granite City' of Aberdeen is probably unique in the British economy in that it has managed to make the leap from one major industry — fishing — to another — oil and gas exploitation — by being able to exploit its position as a major North Sea port. As a consequence, it has managed to retain a greater proportion of its railway infrastructure than many similarly sized cities elsewhere in the United Kingdom. Clearly visible in 'Then' photographs are the passenger station (by this date jointly owned by the LMS and LNER; 1) which is situated on the line north towards Inverness (2) and south towards Dundee (3). Prominent in the centre of the photograph are

the two goods yards: the ex-Caledonian Railway Guild Street (4) and the ex-Great North of Scotland Deeside (5). Immediately adjacent to the ex-GNoSR yard there is a connection to the lines of the Harbour Trustees. One of these lines (7) ran on the north side of the Upper Dock (8) to form a connection with the ex-GNoSR's second goods yard at Waterloo, whilst the second (6) ran along the south side, serving primarily the Provost Blaikie's Quay of the Victoria Dock. Also visible is the western end of the Albert Basin (9).

The first railway to serve Aberdeen was the line from Ferryhill, which opened to Guild Street on 2 August 1850 under the auspices of the Aberdeen (later Caledonian) Railway. The Great North of Scotland Railway entered the city when it opened its line from Kittybrewster to Waterloo on 24 September 1855. Waterloo was to remain the

GNoSR's passenger station until 4 November 1867 when the line linking Kittybrewster with Guild Street was opened along with the new joint station. To the south of the city, the Deeside Railway line to Ballater had already opened — in three phases, the first section to Banchory on 8 September 1853, Banchory-Aboyne on 2 December 1859 and Aboyne-Ballater on 17 October 1866 — and this line was to be operated by the GNoSR from 1866, access being gained via the CR route southwards. Another company to gain access to Aberdeen via the CR route from Kinnaber Junction was the North British Railway, and Aberdeen was to be the northern terminus for the great 'Railway Races to the North' in 1895. The joint station illustrated here was the result of an agreement of 1899 to extend the existing station — which had proved inadequate — with work being largely completed by 1914.

Today, Aberdeen remains — as is clearly evident in the 'Now' photograph — a railway city of some importance. Apart from Waterloo, which remains open for freight but is not visible in either photograph, the city still possesses the curving lines of the (joint) station along with Guild Street goods yard. The ex-GNoSR goods yard at Deeside is also still extant, although this now forms Aberdeen's container terminal. Also still extant are the Clayhills Carriage Sidings to the south of the station on the Down side, although the area has lost the Harbour Trustee lines along the quayside. The only real casualty in terms of the local network has been the demise of the line to Ballater, which lost its passenger services on 28 February 1966 and was to close completely in stages between 18 July 1966

and 1 January 1967. Passenger services are provided by three of the Train Operating Companies, with Virgin Cross Country providing long-distance services to Birmingham and the southwest and Great North Eastern Railway operating over the East Coast main line to Edinburgh and London, with sleeper services and local services north and south being provided by ScotRail. **(60043/687166)**

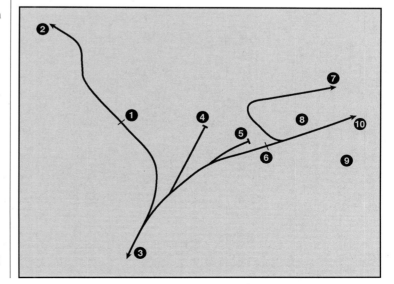

ABINGDON

Then: 3 July 1958
Now: 31 May 2000

When the first of these two photographs was taken, Abingdon was firmly within the county of Berkshire; local government reorganisation in the early 1970s saw the town transferred to Oxfordshire. As will be seen clearly in these two photographs, this is but one change to have affected Abingdon.

The short — two-mile — branch to Radley on the Didcot-Oxford line was opened by the Abingdon Railway Co on 2 June 1856. From the start the line was operated by the Great Western Railway, which took over the

Abingdon company in 1904. Initially the line was broad gauge, but was to be converted to standard gauge in late November 1872.

At the date of the 'Then' photograph, Abingdon was still provided with a passenger service, but this was destined to be withdrawn on 9 September 1963. However, the line was to survive for a further two decades for freight traffic, towards the end primarily for cars produced at the town's MG factory. Unfortunately, production of MG cars in the town ceased in October 1980 and, with the loss of the line's traffic, closure was to follow. The Oxford University Railway Society — now itself but a page in history — organised a farewell train over the branch in 1984, but official closure did not occur until June 1986 after which the line was lifted.

Although the route of the line can still be seen at the Radley end, in Abingdon itself the station site has been cleared and the ubiquitous car park and supermarket have been built.
(A71820/685663)

Located on the former Great Western line north from Oxford towards Birmingham, Banbury's importance as a railway junction grew following the opening of the Great Central main line southwards and of the GWR cut-off route via Aynho Junction. The first of these views dates to the early 1970s, looking northwards, when much of the local railway network had already been eradicated and when all traces of the former LNWR station — Merton Street — had already been removed.

The first railway to reach Banbury was the Birmingham & Oxford (later GWR) that opened from Oxford to Banbury on 2 September 1850; the line was extended northwards towards Birmingham on 1 October 1852. These lines were built to mixed gauge, although most services initially were broad gauge. The broad gauge was abolished north of Oxford on 1 April 1869. The link between the Great Central at Culworth Junction (south of Woodford) and Banbury Junction (just north of the station) opened to freight on 1 June 1900 and to passenger services on 13 August 1900. The ex-GC line closed completely on 5 September 1966. To the north of the station, there was the GC Exchange Yard; the 'Then' photograph shows this shortly before the yard was converted to terminal sidings on 4 October 1971. The Banbury-Cheltenham line — which diverged from the main line at King's Sutton to the south of Banbury — had lost its passenger services on 4 June 1951 and the remaining stub, from King's Sutton to

Adderbury closed completely on 18 August 1969. The LNWR presence in Banbury came to an end with the closure of the Merton Street to Buckingham branch on 2 January 1961 to passenger services and completely, with the exception of Banbury Merton Street itself (which had been retained as a freight terminal), on 2 December 1963. The short spur between Banbury General and Banbury Merton Street — which was located to the southeast of the ex-GWR station — closed on 6 June 1966. The route of the transfer siding between the GWR and LNWR stations can just be identified five years after closure. The final phase in the railway development of Banbury came with the opening of the GWR's direct route via Bicester; this opened to freight traffic on 4 April 1910 and to passenger services on 1 July of the same year.

Today, Banbury station is remarkably unchanged. The station — common in both illustrations — was the result of rebuilding completed in 1958 and represented the first station rebuilt by Western Region following on from the 1955 Modernisation Plan. Freight has all but disappeared, although a small oil terminal serves Dominion Oil on part of the old goods yard to the south of the station on the down side. Another survival from the earlier photograph is the station's semaphore signalling, which continues to be controlled by two manual boxes — North and South — which are clearly visible in both views. The modern Banbury sees passenger services from three TOCs — Chiltern serving the Marylebone-Bicester-Banbury-Birmingham route, Thames Trains operating to Stratford and Virgin Cross Country on the long-distance services. **(A217626/684320)**

BANFF

Then: 6 July 1954
Now: 12 January 2001

Located on the west side of the estuary of the River Deveron, Banff was the terminus of a short branch from Tillynaught Junction station. Built under the aegis of the

Banff, Portsoy & Strathisla Railway, the line, and the associated route from Grange to Portsoy, opened on 30 July 1859. Initially, the BP&SR operated the route itself, but operation was to pass to the Great North of Scotland Railway in February 1863. The singe-track approaches to the branch terminus a Banff are clearly visible in this view looking east towards Banff and,

across the estuary, Macduff. Banff possessed a small single-track engine shed, which is visible at the country end of the platform; this was destined to remain operational until the line's closure. Also visible on the east side of the Deveron is the branch terminus at Macduff; this route was constructed by the GNoSR, opening from Gellymill on 1 July 1872.

At the time of the earlier photograph, Banff was still served by both passenger and freight services, although Macduff had already seen its passenger services withdrawn (on 1 October 1951). A decade later, on 1 August 1961, the Macduff branch was to close completely. It would be a decade after the date of the 'Then' photograph before the Beeching Report listed the Banff route as one to lose its passenger services; these were withdrawn from the branch on 6 July 1964. Freight

facilities continued at Banff until the line's complete closure on 6 May 1968.

Today, the engine shed has disappeared, demolished after closure, and the rest of the site has been cleared. The location of the various station buildings can be identified by careful examination of the excavations in the adjacent hillside, although all physical traces of the actual buildings have long gone. The trackbed along the foreshore has been converted for use as a road although it is possible to identify the still-extant trackbed at the extreme west of the photograph, where it runs inland behind the terrace of houses. Ironically, the trackbed of the Macduff branch can be identified more readily on the east side of the river.

(A55285/687169)

BANGOR

Then: 1920
Now: 13 January 2001

Viewed looking northwards, with the Thomas Telford-designed suspension bridge across the Menai Strait linking the mainland with Anglesey, the London & North Western main line from Chester to Holyhead passes through en route towards the Britannia bridge. Although catalogued by Aerofilms as 'Bangor', the actual station and town of that name are slightly to the north and the station illustrated here is the junction of Menai Bridge. This was the point where the LNWR branch to Caernarfon headed south whilst the main line headed west across the Menai Strait towards Holyhead. This is one of the oldest photographs in the book, almost at the very dawn of aerial photography, and shows the station as it existed in the last days of the pre-Grouping era. Note, in particular, the tank

engine at the head of the goods train at the signalbox. Judging from the angle of steam emerging from the safety valves, the locomotive would appear to be shunting.

The main line from Chester westwards to Bangor was opened by the Chester & Holyhead Railway — later London & North Western — to passenger trains on 1 May 1848 and to freight traffic on 1 June 1848. On the Isle of Anglesey, services commenced between Holyhead and a temporary station at Llanfair on 1 August 1848. Work continued on the Britannia bridge and the first train crossed the Menai Strait on 5 March 1850. Services officially commenced between Bangor and Llanfair through the up side of the bridge on 18 March 1850, with all services using this portion of the bridge until 19 October 1850 when the down side was completed. The branch to the present Caernarfon (at that time Carnarvon, but renamed Caernarvon in 1926) — authorised by the Bangor & Carnarvon Act of 20 May 1851 was inspired by

the potential of the slate traffic. The route opened from Menai Bridge Junction to Port Dinorwic for freight traffic on 10 March 1852. The branch was opened to passenger services through to Caernarfon on 1 July 1852 and to freight on 10 August 1852. The LNWR took over the C&HR on 1 January 1859. The track layout at Menai Bridge was altered in 1870 as a result of an accident on 9 May 1865 when 25 passengers were injured. The line was doubled to Caernarfon between 1872 and 1874.

Menai Bridge lost its passenger services on 14 February 1966 and its freight facilities were withdrawn on 4 March 1968. Passenger services over the route between Menai Bridge Junction and Caernarfon were withdrawn on 5 January 1970 at which time the line closed completely. It had had a brief swansong during the summer of 1969 as a result of the investiture of Prince Charles as Prince of Wales. It was also to

receive a brief resurrection as a result of the fire that seriously damaged the Britannia tubular bridge, when it was reopened for freight traffic. This second life, however, was only to last until the bridge reopened; final closure came on 31 January 1972. Today, the Chester-Holyhead line sees passenger services from a number of TOCs, with long-distance services provided by Virgin West Coast and with local services by First North Western and Wales & West. The possible creation of a new Welsh franchise will, however, potentially see some changes in the future. As can be seen, the suspension bridge stills stands proudly across the straits. In the foreground, shrouded in trees and shadows, the ex-LNWR main line still forms an essential link between Anglesey and the main land. Of the station, however, there is now no trace. **(2042/687180)**

BARKING

Then: 1931
Now: 12 July 2000

Almost 70 years divide the scenes recorded in these two photographs of Barking, in East London. Although much of the surrounding property has altered beyond recognition — even the football pitch has disappeared to be redeveloped — the railway remains a constant feature, despite having been rebuilt.

Barking was and is an important junction on the erstwhile London, Tilbury & Southend Railway and is also served by the District Line of London Underground. These views, taken looking northeastwards, show the eight platform faces of the station to be unchanged over the 70-year period, despite work on remodelling the station in the 1930s and the electrification of the LT&S

route.

The railway first reached Barking on 13 April 1854 with the opening of the line from Forest Gate to Tilbury Fort via Dagenham; the line was jointly promoted by the Eastern Counties and the London & Blackwall railways. Barking became a junction once the cut-off route to Gas Factory Junction (at Bow) was opened on 31 March 1857. This line had been authorised on 7 July 1856. From the date of its opening, trains to Southend operated to Fenchurch Street, although the Eastern Counties (later the GER) continued to run from Barking to Bishopsgate until 1918. The somewhat complex ownership of the line was eventually to be regularised as the London, Tilbury & Southend; following the company's inability to persuade the GER to operate the route, the LT&S started to operate the line itself in the mid-1870s. A further cut-off route, running via Upminster from Barking Tilbury Line Junction East was authorised on 24 July 1882 and opened

on 1 June 1888. The line was quadrupled eastwards to Barking in the first decade of the 20th century, the section between East Ham and Barking being completed in 1908. This allowed for the introduction of District Railway services to the station, these commencing to Barking on 1 April 1908. The District trains were electric-operated and used the northernmost pair of lines into the station. The LT&S was to become part of the Midland Railway on 1 January 1912.

The earlier of these two photographs shows Barking in 1931, immediately before the quadrupling of the line towards Upminster, which was opened on 12 September 1932 and allowed for the extension of District line services eastwards. Note on the road bridge — a level crossing until 1907 — in front of the main station building, the electric tram. In the days before the creation of the London Passenger Transport Board, this is operating over section of tramway controlled by Barking

Urban District Council. These were converted to trolleybus operation in the late 1930s.

Today, Barking continues to see District Line services running to and from Upminster. The majority of main line passenger services through the station are in the hands of the TOC that is the modern-day successor to the LT&SR — c2c — although the solid diet of EMUs represented by that company's services to and from Fenchurch Street is, to an extent, relieved by the DMU shuttle operated by Silverlink to Gospel Oak. The slightly wider angle of the 'Now' shot shows some of the work undertaken to the west of Barking station — in particular the flyover — in connection with the electrification of the LT&SR lines in the late 1950s. Initial electric services were introduced through Barking on 6 November 1961 and a full timetable commenced on 18 June 1962.
(36591/685934)

BARNSLEY

Then: 18 July 1961
Now: 24 January 2001

Dominated by the local coal industry, Barnsley was at the centre of a railway network designed to exploit the wealth extracted from the numerous local collieries. Inevitably the town was to become the focus of the railway ambitions of a number of pre-Grouping companies — the Great Central (as it ultimately became), the Midland and the Lancashire & Yorkshire. This pair of views, taken looking westwards, shows the proximity of the town's two passenger stations. Further from the camera is Barnsley Court House (1); although this was located on the Midland Railway route from Sheffield (8), which terminated at Court House Junction (3) to the north on the

line to Penistone (2), this station was also used by GCR trains, as this company did not possess its own station. Slightly to the east is Barnsley Exchange (6), which was located on the LYR route from Doncaster (7) to Wakefield (5). Just to the west of Exchange station can be seen Barnsley West Junction (9), which also headed towards Court House Junction. Between the two passenger stations can be seen the ex-GCR Barnsley Central goods yard (4). By the date of the 'Then' photograph, passenger services had already ceased at Court House station — succumbing on 19 April 1960 — and Exchange had already reverted to being called Barnsley.

The first line to serve the town was the future LYR, which opened from Horbury, near Wakefield, to the town on 1 January 1850 for passenger services and 15 January 1850 for freight. The future GC reached the town from Mexborough on 1 July 1851. The Manchester, Sheffield & Lincolnshire Railway (later GCR) line from Penistone opened to a station called Regent Street on 1 December 1859; this station was to lose its passenger services in 1870 with the opening of Court House, but was retained as the Central goods yard. The Midland presence in the town came with the opening of the line from Cudworth, which opened on 28 June 1869 for freight and 2 May 1870 for passenger services. This opening resulted in the closure of the line from Court House Junction to Barnsley West Junction on 1 June 1870; the line was reopened on 19 April 1960 as a result of the closure of Court House station. At the same time, the section from Barnsley Court House goods yard to Barnsley West Junction closed completely (although it was still extant in the 'Then' photograph).

Today, Barnsley retains passenger services over the lines towards Penistone — although these were withdrawn on 5 January 1970 only to be reinstated in May 1983 when Sheffield-Huddersfield services were diverted — and between Wakefield and Sheffield. The line through

Court House station was to close completely on 31 January 1966, when the section between Court House junction and Court House goods yard closed. Barnsley Central goods yard closed on 6 November 1967. As can be seen, the scene here is radically different today. All trace of the Court House station platforms and the lines serving them have been eradicated, although the old Court House (incorporated into the station — hence its name) is still extant and provides a reference point to the route of the now-closed line. A new station on the site of the erstwhile Exchange station has been built, linked to a bus station. To the north of the station, at Barnsley Station Junction, the single-track line towards Penistone diverges from the line northwards to Wakefield.
(A93628/687536)

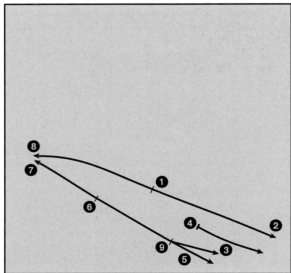

BARNSTAPLE

Then: 8 June 1958
Now: 1 May 2000

The North Devon town of Barnstaple was served by both the Great Western and London & South Western railways; this pair of photographs illustrates the changes wrought to the lines inherited by BR from the latter. The ex-GWR terminus — Victoria Road — was to the right of the picture, located to the southeast of Barnstaple Town station. Visible clearly, however, is Barnstaple Town station (1); until 1935 this was also the terminus of the narrow gauge Lynton & Barnstaple Railway and the curve of the abandoned trackbed can just be seen to the north of the station. Beyond Barnstaple Town, the standard gauge line heads northwards to Ilfracombe (2). Heading north on

the west bank of the river is the line towards Halwill
Junction (3), with Barnstaple Junction station (4) where it
joins the line towards Barnstaple Town. In the foreground,
the line heads south towards Exeter (5); the connection to
the ex-GWR line was just to the south of this point.

The history of the railway development in Barnstaple is
complex, involving as it does railway politics and
problems with gauge between the LSWR — eager to
expand beyond Exeter — and the GWR. Eventually, the
line was to be constructed to the broad gauge and was
opened between Barnstaple and the Exeter & Crediton
Railway on 12 July 1854; it was extended to Bideford on
2 November 1855. However, in 1862/63 the LSWR took
over the leases of the Exeter & Crediton, the North Devon
and the Bideford Extension railways and the track was
converted to mixed gauge operation. The last broad gauge
train reached Bideford in 1877. The extension across the
river to Ilfracombe was opened on 20 July 1874.

Today, railway facilities at Barnstaple have diminished
significantly. Passenger services at Victoria Road ceased
on 13 June 1960 with trains diverted to Barnstaple
Junction until closure of the line on 3 October 1966.
Victoria Road was retained as a goods depot, latterly
accessed via the LSWR route, until closure on 5 March
1970. The Barnstaple-Torrington line lost its passenger
services on 4 October 1965 (the section between
Torrington and Halwill had closed earlier in the year),
although the section from Barnstaple and Bideford was
reopened for a fortnight in January 1968 to provide access
as a result of damage to a road bridge. The line from
Barnstaple Junction to Ilfracombe, including Barnstaple
Town, lost its passenger services on 5 October 1970, at
which time the line closed completely. There were half-
hearted efforts to try and preserve the line, but these came

to nothing. Finally the freight-only line beyond Barnstaple
to Bideford, Torrington and Meeth closed completely from
5 March 1983. As can be seen from the more recent
photograph, the trackbed of the Bideford Extension
Railway is still clearly identifiable beyond the much
reduced station at Barnstaple Junction. Little, however,
now remains to remind people that the railway once
crossed the river — the bridge has been demolished —
and again much of the former railway land is now
occupied by car parks and retail units.
(A71438/685311)

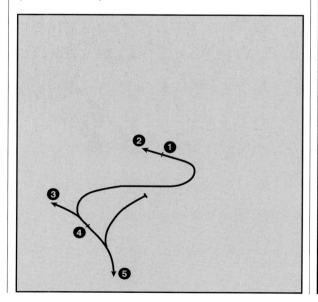

BARNT GREEN

Woodbridge. The second route to serve Beccles was the Waveney Valley Railway, which was built to provide a link via Bungay to Tivetshall on the Norwich-Ipswich main line. Although the first section of the WVR was opened on 1 December 1855, it was not until 2 March 1863 that the section from Bungay to Beccles was completed.

The earlier of these two photographs, taken looking northwards, shows clearly the station at Beccles along with its associated facilities. Slightly to the north of the station, the Waveney Valley line heads westwards to Bungay and thence to Tivetshall. Passenger services over the WVR had already been withdrawn, on 5 January 1953, and on 15 November 1954 a Light Railway Order covering the route was issued. However, further closures were to follow, with the complete closure of the section from Bungay to Harleston on 1 February 1960, thus by the date of the first illustration, the WVR had been

effectively reduced at its eastern end to a branch linking Bungay with Beccles.

Rationalisation is the order of the day at Beccles as is made abundantly clear in the more recent photograph. The Bungay line closed in two stages: from Ditchingham to Bungay on 3 August 1964 and Beccles to Ditchingham on 19 April 1965. Today, there is no trace of the existence of the branch. The East Suffolk line, despite being threatened with closure, remains, although the facilities have been much reduced. The line has been singled north of Halesworth, much of the work being undertaken in the early 1980s when the line was used to pioneer the introduction the concept of radio control from a single signalbox. The single track can be seen snaking its way through the somewhat basic station at Beccles. Currently, services are provided by Anglia Railways, with just under 10 return workings per weekday.
(A111213/685093)

BIRMINGHAM

Then: 5 June 1964
Now: 30 April 2000

These two views of Birmingham, taken almost 40 years apart, are instructive in that the first was taken contemporaneously with the redevelopment of the city centre, which resulted in the construction of the Bull Ring shopping centre and the reconstruction of New Street station whilst the more modern shot records the era when Birmingham's city centre was again under redevelopment. Looking southwards, clearly visible are two of the city's central stations New Street (1) in the distance and Moor Street (2) in the foreground. Moor Street is situated on the ex-Great Western main line from Tyseley (3) towards Snow Hill (4) whilst in the foreground the ex-London & North Western Railway line from Coventry (6) can be seen entering the 254yd-long New Street South Tunnel (5).

New Street was the joint Midland/London & North Western Railway station serving the city; first called 'New Street' in 1852 (with the opening of Snow Hill), it was officially opened in 1854. The station was effectively divided in two, the MR section to the south and the LNWR section to the north. The latter lost its overall roof in 1946, this being replaced by platform awnings, although by 1963 — shortly before the date of the 'Then' photograph — work had commenced on the complete

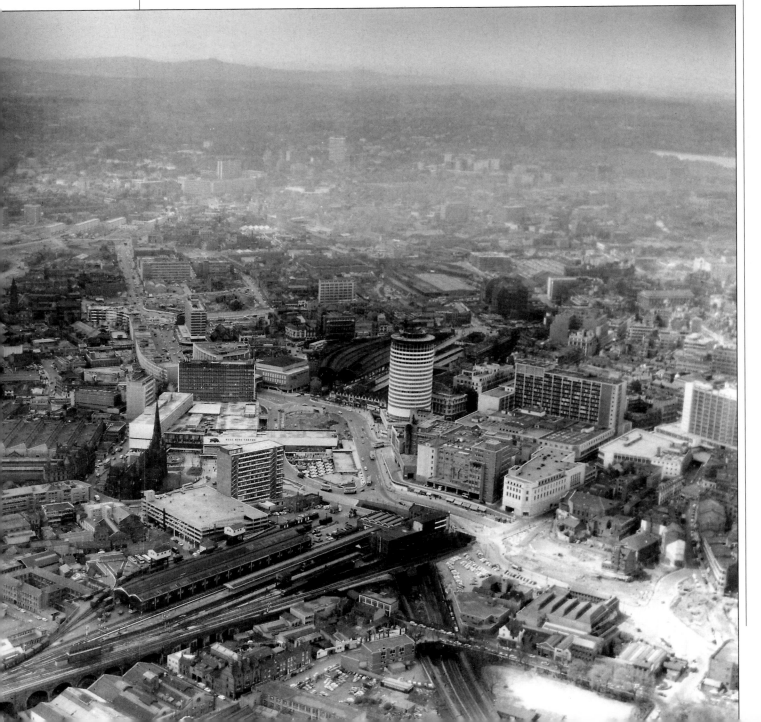

rebuilding of the station. The GWR route through Birmingham opened from the south to Snow Hill on 1 October 1852; the station was officially known as 'Snow Hill' from February 1858. The station at Moor Street, however, was not to open until 1907 when it effectively provided Snow Hill's southern terminal platforms in order to relieve congestion on the section into Snow Hill proper; when first built, Moor Street did not possess platforms on the through lines towards Snow Hill.

Today, there would appear to be much continuity between the railway scene of 1964 and that of the 21st century. In reality, however, much has changed in the intervening period. The ex-LNWR lines into New Street station have been electrified — services commencing on 5 December 1966 — and New Street station itself has been completely rebuilt. The areas surrounding the station are, however, undergoing further redevelopment; after nearly 40 years the Bull Ring complex is being demolished and rebuilt; unfortunately, the opportunity is not being taken during this redevelopment to try and widen the eastern approaches to New Street station. At the time of the 'Then' photograph, the ex-GWR lines were witnessing a swan-song, as traffic was diverted away from the ex-LNWR route in order to relieve pressure during the electrification process. Once completed, however, the gradual elimination of the ex-GWR route commenced. Through trains were withdrawn in March 1967 and on 4 March 1968 all services from the south terminated at Moor Street, allowing for the complete closure of the section through Snow Hill Tunnel. However, on 4 October 1987 the line through the tunnel was restored and passenger services diverted from Moor Street to a new terminus at Snow Hill. The original Moor Street station

was closed and platforms, for the first time, installed on the through lines. Originally, it had been planned that the canopies from Moor Street would be transferred to the new Severn Valley Railway station at Kidderminster, but this proposal did not proceed. As can be seen, some 13 years after closure, Moor Street retains its platforms and canopies (although the railway land to the north is being redeveloped as part of the new Bull Ring scheme) and current proposals by Chiltern Trains, as part of their franchise renegotiations, envisage restoring the currently disused platforms at Moor Street to use.
(A126638/685100)

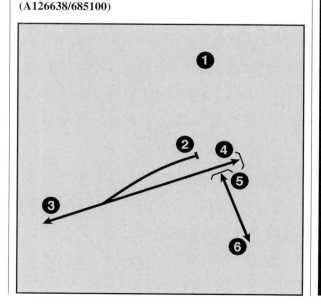

BLACKBURN

Taken looking northeastwards, this pair of photographs shows the close proximity of three forms of transport: the Leeds-Liverpool Canal (opened in 1816) being visible to the east of the railway station whilst immediately to the west of the station buses can be seen from the Corporation fleet. It was only five years earlier that Blackburn had bidden farewell to the last of its 4ft 0in gauge electric trams and close examination of the area in front of the station in the 'Then' photograph shows the former tram track still extant and awaiting removal. The first of these two photographs shows clearly the extent of the railway station and goods yard serving this important Lancashire mill centre in the years immediately after Nationalisation. All the lines serving Blackburn were eventually to form part of the Lancashire & Yorkshire Railway's network before passing, via the London & North Western in 1922, to the LMSR in 1923.

The Blackburn & Preston Railway was the first to serve the town, opening on 1 June 1846; it was extended eastwards to Accrington on 19 June 1848 under the notional auspices of the East Lancashire Railway (which had merged with the Blackburn & Preston in July 1845). The next phase came with the amalgamation of two earlier railways promoting lines to serve Blackburn into the pithily titled Bolton, Blackburn, Clitheroe & West Yorkshire Railway on 9 July 1847. The line south from Blackburn towards Darwen opened on 3 August 1847 and that north towards Clitheroe followed on 20 June 1850, although it would not be completed through to Hellifield for a further 30 years. The BBC&WYR originally had its own station in Blackburn, which was closed in 1858 as part of the process by which the L&YR gradually took over operation and control of the various lines. The trainshed illustrated in the first of these two photographs dates from the remodelling of the station in the late 1880s as does the main station building, which was completed in 1888.

Work commenced on the redevelopment of Blackburn station in the late 1990s and, as can be seen, involved the removal of the original roof and platform canopies. Although the platforms remained as did the buildings at ground level facing the bus station, new facilities are being constructed on platforms 1 to 3. Apart from the main station buildings (which had undergone modernisation in the early 1980s), the large goods shed is also still extant, although no longer rail served, and the sidings to the east — the East Lancashire Sidings — survive in part. Today, Blackburn remains an important railway junction, particularly given the restoration of passenger services over the line northwards to Hellifield. The majority of passenger services through the station are provided by the trans-Pennine services of Northern Spirit between Blackpool and the West Riding of Yorkshire and by First North Western on the routes from Manchester to Clitheroe via Bolton and from Preston to Colne. **(R20501/687365)**

BLYTH

Then: 6 July 1964
Now: 12 January 2001

One of the constant themes through this book is how far the decline of Britain's traditional industries has resulted in the diminution of the railway network. One of the regions to be severely affected by the disappearance of the coal industry is the northeast of England and no place illustrates this better than Blyth in Northumberland. This pair of views shows how dramatic the changes have been over the past four decades. Taken looking northeastwards with the North Sea in the background, the estuary of the River Blyth formed a harbour from which much of the region's coal industry was shipped by sea southwards. To serve the local coal industry an intricate network of lines

was constructed by the North Eastern Railway and its antecedents on both banks of the river, evidence of which is clearly visible in the 'Then' shot which shows, in the foreground, the line serving Blyth station with its extension through to the south bank of the river and, in the background, the vast array of sidings and coal staiths serving the north bank.

The line serving Blyth — which became formalised as part of the Blyth & Tyne Railway by an Act of 30 June 1852 and then part of the NER in 1874 — was opened between Seghill Colliery and Blyth for freight in 1846 and to passenger services on 3 March 1847. In 1850 a further line, from Newsham to Bedlington, opened resulting in the Blyth line becoming a branch off the route at Newsham. A second line from Newsham serving staiths to the south of the area illustrated here opened in the 1880s. The line serving Blyth North was the result of considerable expansion in the facilities provided at Blyth and was an extension of the 1867 line that served Cambois. The North Eastern Railway opened to the new staiths on 13 July 1896. This was not the final expansion in the facilities offered at Blyth, as further expansion continued post-World War 1. The scene in the 'Then' shot records the era shortly after the period when Blyth had

shipped out its maximum annual tonnage (in 1961 the harbour despatched almost 6.9m tons of coal). However, not all was rosy; Blyth was to lose its passenger services shortly after the date of the 'Then' photograph (on 2 November 1964).

Also visible in the 'Then' photograph are the two locomotive sheds that served Blyth: South (in the foreground) and North (across the river). South shed dated originally to 1880 and was extended in 1894. Facilities included a turntable and coaling stage; the shed closed on 28 May 1967. North opened in 1897 and was to close on 9 September 1967.

Today, the picture is a very different one to that recorded 37 years ago. The site of the station and South shed has been completely redeveloped and there is now no evidence that the railway once provided the town with a branch. The second route from Newsham Junction, to the south of this area, to Blyth is, however, still operational. To the north of the river, Blyth North shed has also been demolished and the numerous sidings that once served the staiths have been lifted. There is, however, still railway activity slightly to the north, with an import terminal for Alcan and other facilities around the Cambois area. **(A134186/687379)**

Then: 21 April 1972
Now: 4 March 2000

The Sussex coastal town and resort of Bognor Regis came to prominence during the reign of King George V when the king made use of its facilities for recuperation after illness. Although the town gained its 'Regis' suffix in 1929 as a result of these regal visits, the king himself is renowned for being slightly less complimentary.

The railway first reached the town with the opening of the London, Brighton & South Coast Railway branch from Barnham Junction on 1 June 1864. The line was originally constructed as a single track and was doubled during the first decade of the 20th century. The station was rebuilt in 1902. The line to Bognor Regis was electrified as part of the 'Portsmouth Number Two' project and new electric services were introduced on 2 July 1938. The first of these two photographs shows the state of Bognor Regis station and its environs in the early 1970s, by which time the service was dominated by EMUs painted in the blue and white livery of that era.

Today, the scene Bognor Regis is largely unchanged. The 1902 station remains, as do the EMUs, although the latter are now under the control (at the time of writing) of Connex South Central. Freight facilities have, as with so many other places, been withdrawn and the site redeveloped, although the goods shed remains standing. Other changes include the rearrangement of the station forecourt with the demolition of the single-storey parade of shops.
(A229684/684253)

BOLTON

Then: 19 May 1964
Now: 10 January 2001

Viewed looking southwards, this pair of photographs records the ex-Lancashire & Yorkshire Railway engine shed at Bolton (3), which was situated on the line between Manchester (1) and Bolton (Trinity Street) (2). Adjacent to the shed was a wagon repair works (4) whilst in the distance the line towards Bury can be seen heading eastwards (5) from Bolton East Junction (7). In the foreground of the 'Then' photograph, the goods yard to the south of Bolton station is evident (6). The shed was built in two phases, with the first four-road section being opened in 1874 as a replacement for an earlier shed located adjacent to the station. The shed was extended in

1888 by the addition of a further eight-road structure. It was also in 1888 that the turntable and coaling stage with water tank were added. The shed as illustrated in the earlier of the two photographs had been reroofed by the LMS during 1946.

Although destined to become the pivotal part of the railway network serving Bolton, the L&YR main line illustrated here was not the first railway to serve Bolton; that honour went to the Bolton & Leigh (later LNWR), which opened its first section on 1 August 1828. The LNWR line was to be served throughout its life by a separate terminus in the town, Great Moor Street. The main line illustrated here owes its origins to a decision taken in 1831 by the Manchester, Bolton & Bury Canal Co to replace its existing canal with a railway line. In the event, the company — now graced with the snappy title of the Manchester, Bolton & Bury Canal Navigation & Railway — decided to build its railway line alongside the canal, opening on 29 May 1845. The line towards Bury was promoted by the Liverpool & Bury Railway, which was incorporated on 31 July 1845 and which opened on 20 November 1848, by which time it had become part of the L&YR.

Bolton shed was closed completely on 1 July 1968 and was demolished after closure; today the site has been completely redeveloped. Another casualty is the line towards Bury; this lost its passenger service on 5 October 1970, at which time the line between Bolton East Junction to Bury closed completely. The section of line in the foreground remains four-track, although the goods yard is now out of use and weed strewn. Local passenger services between Manchester and Bolton are in the hands of First North Western.
(A127940/687380)

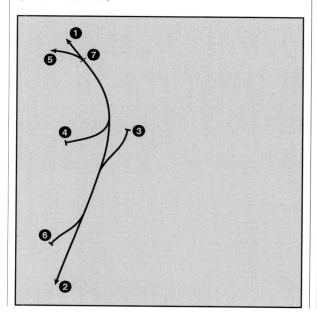

BRAINTREE

Then: 1965
Now: 16 April 2000

At the time of the 'Then' photograph, the station was known as 'Braintree & Bocking' although today it is simply Braintree. The branch from Witham opened under the aegis of the Maldon, Witham & Braintree Railway for freight on 15 August 1848 and to passenger services on the following 2 October. The original station was sited where the goods yard is located in the 'Then' photograph; the passenger station was relocated on 22 February 1869 with the opening of the 18-mile long line to Bishop's Stortford. By the date of the first photograph, passenger services had already succumbed on the line towards Bishop's Stortford, having been

itself closed on 28 November 1977). Passenger services between Bridgend and Barry were withdrawn on 15 June 1964 and those between Bridgend and Tondu (thence to Treherbert) were to follow on 15 June 1970. Both the Barry and Tondu lines were, however, to survive for freight and passenger services were restored between Bridgend and Maesteg on 28 September 1992. Today, passenger services operate through the station under the auspices of First Great Western and Virgin Cross-Country on express services, whilst Wales & West provide local trains.
(8638/684276)

BRIDGWATER

Viewed looking eastwards, this shows part of the Somerset port of Bridgwater and the area between part of the docks and the ex-Great Western main line, which can be seen running from north to south in the background. In the first of these two photographs, a branch can be seen heading westwards from the main line over a bridge towards the foreground; this was the ex-GWR line serving the docks at Bridgwater. The Tidal Basin for the docks can be seen in the extreme left hand corner at the bottom. To the north of the long hipped building — situated between the river and the main line — can just be distinguished the roof of the terminus of the Somerset & Dorset Joint branch, Bridgwater North. The S&DJR branch from Edington opened on 21 July 1890 under the aegis of the

independent Bridgwater Railway. The branch passed over the ex-GWR main line slightly to the north of the scene illustrated here. Passenger services over the branch ceased on 1 December 1952; Bridgwater North continued to serve as a freight yard following complete closure of the branch on 4 October 1954 via a new spur laid into the docks branch, but this had closed by the mid-1960s. The Bridgwater docks were opened on 24 March 1841 and, on 14 June of the same year, trains of the Bristol & Exeter Railway first reached the town. The line opened from Bridgwater to Taunton on 1 July 1842. The line connecting the main line to the docks was constructed partially over an established horse tramway after the GWR acquired the docks as part of its purchase of the Bridgwater & Taunton Canal. The bridge over the river was unusual in that it was a telescopic draw bridge.

Today, Bridgwater is still served by the ex-GWR main line, with long distance services operated through the station by Virgin Cross-Country and First Great Western, and local services in the hands of Wales & West. However, elsewhere there has been considerable change. The area once occupied by the Tidal Pool has been filled in and is now occupied by housing. Whilst it is possible to trace the route of the harbour branch, this closed in 1967 and its route has been largely taken over by a new road. Originally, the old railway bridge was used for road access across the river but this has subsequently been replaced by the structure alongside it. Of the erstwhile Bridgwater North, there is now no trace; the station building was demolished in early August 1984.
(A167314/684263)

BRIDPORT

Although the popular perception is, perhaps, that railway closures were largely a product of the period before and after Beeching, with 1970 almost representing a cut-off point, there were a number of lines that did succumb in the years after 1970, including the branch to the Dorset town of Bridport. This line was to disappear in the mid-1970s and this pair of shots illustrates clearly how quickly, even with a relatively recent closure, all traces of the railway can be eliminated.

The first of this pair of photographs, taken looking the south, shows the station in August 1928, shortly after the Grouping, and portrays clearly the facilities available at

Bridport station. In the foreground the branch heads east towards Maiden Newton and, beyond the station, the single-track line heads towards West Bay. The station is provided with two platforms, up and down, with, adjacent to the Down platform, the small single-track engine shed. On the Up side there was the goods shed and yard, which, in 1928, were doing good business.

The branch to Bridport was opened under the auspices of the Bridport Railway as a broad-gauge line from Maiden Newton. The route was converted to standard gauge in 1871 and taken over by the Great Western Railway in 1901. The branch was extended from Bridport to West Bay — initially called Bridport Harbour — on 31 March 1884, although, by the date of the 'Then' photograph, passenger services over the section from Bridport to West Bay — suspended during World War 1 — were again under threat; they were finally to be withdrawn on 22 September 1930 although the line remained open for freight thereafter. The engine shed was opened on 12 November 1857 and was to survive until 15 June 1959; it was demolished shortly thereafter.

Today, casual viewers would be hard pressed to realise that a branch line had once served this town although, as elsewhere (and out of site of the camera), there has been significant population growth over the past few decades. The site of the station has been completely redeveloped and the route of the line towards West Bay has been incorporated into a new road. The closure of the route came gradually. Freight services between West Bay and Bridport were withdrawn on 3 December 1962. Freight services to Bridport were to be withdrawn on 5 April 1965 and the signalbox closed two months later. For the next decade, Bridport was to be served by passenger services alone, DMUs trundling between it and the Weymouth-Yeovil line at Maiden Newton. Even these were not sacrosanct, as BR announced that the line would close from 3 October 1966. However, consent to closure was refused and for a further nine years the line was to continue in service. Despite this reprieve, threats to the line continued and the final passenger services were withdrawn on 5 May 1975. Track recovery started in November the same year. **(24041/687552)**

BRISTOL

With the through platforms at Bristol Temple Meads (1) in the foreground alongside the original Brunel-designed terminus of the Great Western Railway (2), this dramatic view of Bristol looking westwards shows clearly the ex-GWR main line running past Bath Road depot (3) and Bristol West Junction (10) where the avoiding line comes in from North Somerset Junction (4) before heading westwards past Pyle Hill goods yard (5) and Bedminster station (6) before disappearing in the direction of Taunton (7). Also illustrated (8) are the lines heading towards the north of Temple Meads station and the freight route (9) that bisected the city en route towards the docks and Ashton Junction on the line towards Portishead.

The first railway to serve Bristol was the Bristol & Gloucester Railway, later part of the Midland Railway, which opened to a station at Avonside Wharf on 6 August 1835. Brunel's GWR opened from Bath to the terminus at Temple Meads on 31 August 1840, to be followed by the opening of the Bristol & Exeter line westwards on 1 June 1841. Initially B&ER trains operated into the original Brunel terminus, by reversing, but this arrangement proved unsatisfactory and the B&ER opened its own station at Temple Meads. It was in 1865 that powers were obtained for the construction of a joint station with work commencing in 1871, resulting in the demolition of the B&ER station. The new station, designed largely by Sir Matthew Digby Wyatt, was opened on 1 January 1878. The new station proved inadequate from the start, although it was not until 1929 that work commenced to extend it; the enlarged station was completed by December 1935.

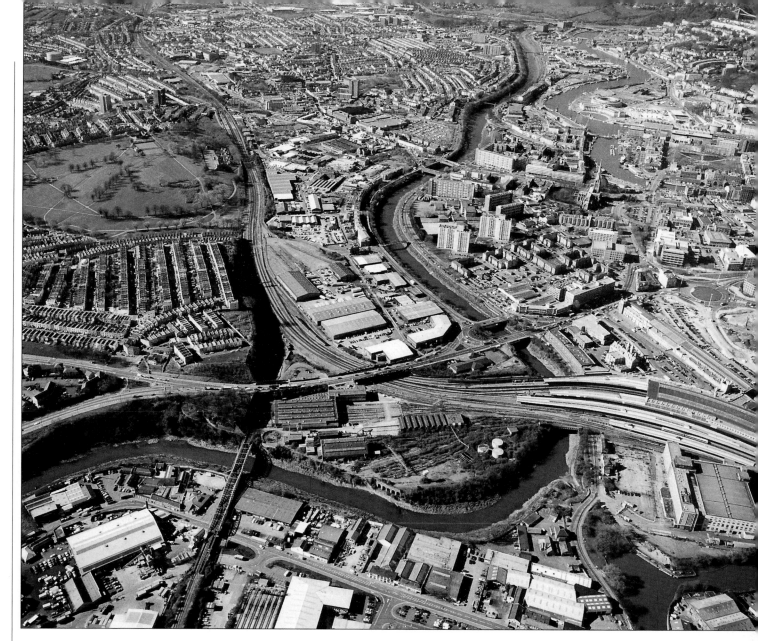

Bristol Bath Road shed owed its origins to a structure first opened by the B&ER in 1850 and extended in both 1859 and 1877. The original locomotive shed was demolished from 1933 onwards and replaced by a new shed by the GWR in 1934. This became coded 82A by British Railways. The shed was to close to steam on 12 September 1960 and was largely demolished to allow for the construction of the diesel depot illustrated here.

Today, Bristol remains a vitally important railway centre, although there has been the inevitable diminution of facilities. The original Brunel terminus is still extant, although no longer in railway use (it has been converted to a museum dedicated to the British Empire). The joint station is, however, still a major focal point for both long distance and local traffic. The avoiding line as well as the main line remain active, although Bath Road shed now stands empty, devoid of activity, its tracks weed-strewn and out of use. Another casualty has been the line from Temple Meads towards the dock area; this was to close completely between Temple Meads and Wapping Wharf on 6 October 1963. Whilst there is still track serving part of the dockside area, this is currently severed at the Ashton Junction end and any railway activity is limited to the services run by the Bristol Industrial Museum. Also now closed is the Pyle Hill

goods yard, although the site has not as yet been redeveloped completely.
(A107024/684280)

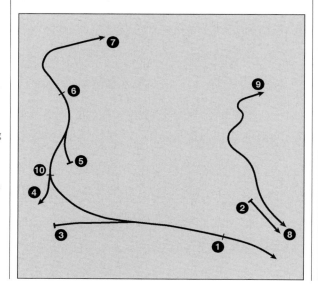

BURTON ON TRENT

Then: 26 April 1947
Now: 19 April 2000

Mention the name Burton to the cognoscenti and it can only mean one thing — the centre of Britain's brewing industry and the home of such classic brewers as Bass. Inevitably a massive network of lines was built both to supply the raw materials for the brewing industry and also to remove the finished product to its market. Although Burton was primarily a Midland Railway town — and the MR transported vast quantities of beer to London — the town was also served by the Great Northern, North Staffordshire and, to a limited extent, by the London & North Western railways. This pair of photographs, taken

looking northwards, shows how radically the railway presence has altered in Burton over the past 50 years. The scale of the sidings and warehouses in 1947 are evident as is the complex network of lines that served them. Running from Burton station in the south (1) towards Derby (2) in the north is the Midland main line from Birmingham Arriving from the northwest is the North Staffordshire route from Uttoxeter (3) which passes through Stretton Junction (11) where the LNWR branch serving Horninglow (15) headed south. Passing through the already closed Horninglow station (10; closed 1 January 1949), the ex-NSR route joined the MR line at North Stafford Junction (9). A spur from the NSR line passed over the MR route to the north of the junction connecting, via North Junction (7) with the ex-GNR goods yard at

Hawkins Lane (6) and with the MR Hay branch (5) at Hawkins Lane Junction (8). Further south on the MR line, at Horninglow Junction (13), the ex-MR freight branch to Horninglow Wharf heads west (14), whilst at Guild Street Junction (12), the ex-MR Guild Street branch heads east (4). The Guild Street and Hay branches form a loop slightly to the east of the area illustrated here.

The first railway to serve Burton was the Birmingham & Derby Junction (later part of the Midland), which opened its line south from Derby to Hampton in Arden on 12 August 1839. The North Staffordshire line from Uttoxeter opened on 11 September 1848; it was over this route that the GNR gained access to the town from its Nottingham-Derby line on 1 April 1878. The line from Stretton Junction to North Junction opened in 1868.

Today, the scene at Burton is radically different. Although the brewing industry remains vitally important, the railway's contribution to the industry has largely ceased. The ex-MR line between Derby and Birmingham remains operational. However, the ex-NSR route through Horninglow has closed; passenger services over the route ceased on 13 June 1960. The section from Horninglow Junction to Stretton Junction closed completely on 30 January 1967 and that between Hawkins Lane Junction and Eggington, via North Junction and Stretton Junction, followed on 6 May 1968. The ex-MR branch to Horninglow Wharf closed on 28 February 1969, whilst the ex-GNR goods yard at Hawkins Lane lost its general freight facilities on 6 June 1966 and the ex-LNWR goods yard at Horninglow Street closed on 1 January 1968.

From the air it is evident that much of the former railway land has been redeveloped and it is now almost impossible to identify the location of many of the railway features that existed in 1947. One survivor, however, is the large warehouse (16), which stands alongside the New Wetmore sidings. At this point the main line is still provided with four tracks and limited siding facilities are provided on both the Up and Down side.
(R8170/685108)

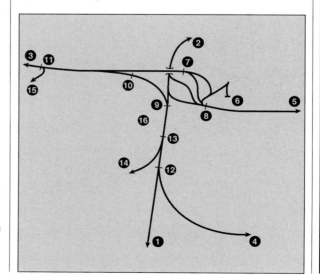

BURY

Then: May 1935
Now: 30 April 2000

The Lancashire town of Bury affords us a great variety in the comparison over a 70-year period as both preservation and the Manchester Metrolink provide subtle changes to the scene. Taken looking northeastwards, the 'Then' photograph provides an excellent overview of the complex network of junctions around Bury Knowsley Street (1) and its adjacent goods shed (2). Knowsley Street station was situated on the line between Bolton (5) and Heywood (3). A second line runs from Rawtenstall in the north (6), via Bury Bolton Street station (not illustrated) towards Manchester (4). From East Lancashire Junction (7) a spur linked to the Bolton-Bury route at Bury West Junction (10). A second spur, from Bury Loop Junction (11) to Bury Loco Junction (12) allowed traffic to run from the

Manchester line towards the Heywood route. In the area to the east of the Manchester-Bolton Street route is situated Bury shed (8) and Buckley Wells carriage shed (9), that was used at this time to house the EMUs for the service between Manchester and Bury.

The first line to serve the region was the Manchester, Bury & Rawtenstall, which obtained its Act on 4 July 1844. It formed part of the East Lancashire Railway on 21 July 1845 and was opened from Clifton to Rawtenstall on 28 September 1846. The line from Castleton had opened under the aegis of the Manchester & Leeds Railway — later Lancashire & Yorkshire — in 1841. The line was extended through to Bury on 1 May 1848 and thence towards Bolton on the following 20 November. To the north of Bolton Street station a branch headed northwestwards to Holcombe Brook; this was opened on 6 November 1882 and was electrified (at 3kV) on 29 July 1913. The Manchester-Bury line was electrified by the

L&YR (as successor to the original East Lancashire Railway) at 1,200V dc on 16 April 1916. Bury shed replaced an earlier structure in 1876. The shed was to be closed by BR on 12 November 1965 and, after a period in use for the storage of electric locomotives, was demolished.

Today, the scene is considerably changed. The carriage shed at Buckley Wells now forms part of the facilities of the preserved East Lancashire Railway and a second shed, further to the north has also been built. The line from Bury Loco Junction to Bolton Street station lost its passenger services on 17 March 1980, when services were diverted into the new Bury Interchange station. The new station was accessed via part of the old line from Bury Loco Junction (which had closed on 24 March 1967) along with a new spur into the town centre. Passenger services between Crumpsall and Bury Interchange were withdrawn on 17 August 1991 to allow for construction of the Manchester Metrolink network, which opened the following year. The line from Castleton via Bury West Junction towards Bolton lost its passenger services on 5 October 1970, at which time the line west from West Junction to Bolton closed completely; there is now virtually no evidence that this line ever existed at this point. Passenger services were withdrawn north of Bolton Street station on 2 June 1972, although the line remained open for freight to Rawtenstall until 8 April 1981, when it was acquired for preservation by the East Lancashire Railway. The line eastwards to Castleton via Heywood

remained open to freight until 4 April 1981 and this route has also been secured for preservation by the ELR. The Holcombe Brook branch lost its passenger services on 8 May 1952, although it had reverted to steam operation for the last year of operation; it was to close completely north of Tottington on 2 May 1960 and south of Tottington to the Rawtenstall line on 19 August 1963. (47494/685114)

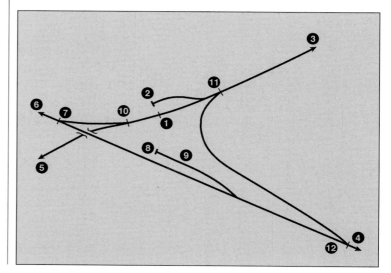

CAERNARFON

Then: 20 July 1961
Now: 13 January 2001

Viewed looking eastwards, this pair of photographs shows the northern end of the station at Caernarfon. The extensive freight facilities and the impressive station buildings are readily apparent in the 'Then' photograph.

The first railway to reach Caernarfon was the branch sponsored by the Chester & Holyhead Railway under the auspices of the Bangor & Carnarvon Railway Act of 20 May 1851. The line opened between Menai Bridge Junction and Port Dinorwic on 10 March 1852 for freight — primarily slate — traffic and through to Caernarfon on 1 July 1852 (passenger) and 10 August 1852 (freight). On 1 January 1859 the London & North Western took over

the C&HR. Although Caernarfon was, at this time, still a branch terminus, there had been proposals for some years to construct an extension southwards. There had been a narrow gauge line — the Nantlle Railway — running south of the town since 1828, but several schemes for the incorporation of this into a new standard gauge route were proposed from the early 1850s onwards. The line — under the auspices of the Carnarvonshire Railway opened from Afon Wen, on the Pwllheli line, to a terminus south of the River Seiont on 2 September 1867. Initially, the line was operated by the Cambrian Railways, but in 1870 the Carnarvonshire Railway was vested in the LNWR. The station as illustrated here was modified in 1869 in order to accommodate the construction of the Caernarfon town line, which linked the two sections of LNWR route and which opened to freight services on 5 July 1870 and to passenger trains in the following January.

When the 'Then' photograph was taken, passenger services continued to run south of the town; however, the line to Afon Wen lost its passenger services on 7 December 1964 at which time the line south from Caernarfon closed completely. Passenger services over the route between Menai Bridge Junction and Caernarfon were withdrawn on 5 January 1970 at which time the line closed completely. It had had a brief swansong during the summer of 1969 as a result of the investiture of Prince Charles as Prince of Wales, a ceremony which was held at Caernarfon Castle. The line was also to be reopened temporarily for freight traffic as a result of serious fire damage to the Britannia bridge at Bangor, but this was to be a shortlived reprieve and final closure came on 31 January 1972. Today, a new railway age has dawned at Caernarfon with the opening of part of the revived Welsh Highland Railway from the south, which runs over the erstwhile standard gauge line from Dinas Junction. However, the new FR station is to the south of the original LNWR station in the town and, as is clearly evident from the 'Now' photograph, all traces of the standard gauge line at this point have been removed. The location of the station is easily identifiable by reference to the surviving terraces of houses beyond the site, but of the station and goods yard, there is now no trace.
(A93082/687387)

CAERPHILLY

Then: 26 September 1961
Now: 1 May 2000

Located in the Welsh Valleys between Rhymney and Cardiff, Caerphilly was an important strategic location — witness the mediaeval castle in the foreground — long before it became the location of an important railway

junction and locomotive works. These views, taken looking east, show the changes wrought in this community over the past 40 years. From the west comes the line from Rhymney (2) passing through Caerphilly station (1) en route to East Branch Junction (3), where the line divides. The main line headed eastwards towards Cardiff and entering the 1 mile 181yd-long Caerphilly Tunnel (4) with the branch heading north towards Machen

(5). Slightly to the east of the junction is Caerphilly Works (6).

All the lines illustrated here were initially owned by the Rhymney Railway, passing to the GWR in 1923, although the line towards Machen was owned by the Brecon & Merthyr beyond an end-on junction (7). Backed by the Bute family — who did much to promote the development of the South Wales coal and railway industry — the Rhymney Railway's original main line was opened between Cardiff and Rhymney to freight on 25 February 1858 and on 31 March 1858 to passenger services; this line ran to the west of the town and is thus out of frame. The lines illustrated here were authorised by acts in the early 1860s. The line towards Machen opened for coal traffic in 1864, but passenger services were not introduced — due to the gradients — until 28 December 1887 and, at the Machen end, a loop was opened on 14 September 1891 to alleviate the gradients encountered on the original alignment. The line towards Cardiff opened on 1 April 1871 at which time the station illustrated here was opened. By the date of the 'Then' photograph, passenger services over the route to Machen had already been withdrawn — on 17 September 1956 — but the line remained open for freight traffic.

Caerphilly Works was opened in 1899 and replaced the Rhymney Railway's earlier workshops at Cardiff Docks. Apart from the locomotive works, which handled the overhaul of locomotives but not their construction, the site also included carriage repair shops; the Carriage & Wagon Works opened in 1901, although work on the latter was transferred to Cardiff Cathays in 1930. The carriage shops are towards the west of the site and the locomotive works towards the east. Inevitably, with the contraction of the railway industry after Nationalisation small workshops like Caerphilly were uneconomic and the locomotive works was to close shortly after the date of the 'Then'

photograph on 29 June 1963. The Carriage Works had already ceased to handle work — in May 1962 — but work was still being undertaken on DMUs.

Today, Caerphilly is a much reduced railway location. The station, rebuilt in 1974, posseses two platform faces. East of the station, the line towards Machen is now no more, having closed completely on 20 November 1967. Although part of works is still extant, the site — once known as the Harold Wilson Industrial Estate — has been largely cleared. The Caerphilly Railway Society maintained a presence on the site for some years, although this has now closed.
(A96330/685117)

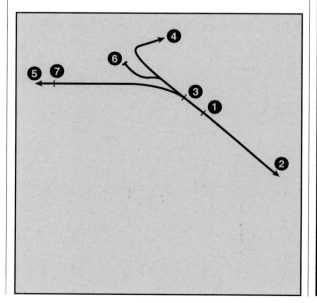

CARDIFF

Then: 1930s
Now: 1 May 2000

One of the constant themes through this book is the close relationship between Britain's traditional heavy industries — coal, iron, steel and shipbuilding — and the railways and how far the decline in the former has led to a contraction in the latter. There are few locations that demonstrate this inter-relationship better than South Wales, and Cardiff in particular. A period of more than 60 years separates these two photographs and, in that period, a complete transformation has been wrought; there are the odd common factors, such as the ex-Great Western main line running from west to east, but the sheer scale of the railway infrastructure in the 1930s is almost unimaginable today.

The scene illustrated in the first of these two photographs shows the network of lines that served Bute East Dock (7) in the 1930s, when much of the region's traditional industry was still routed through the numerous docks of Cardiff. Illustrated are lines inherited by the LMS from the London & North Western Railway and by the expanded GWR from the Cardiff and Rhymney railways as well as from the original Great Western. Running from east (2) to west (3) is the Great Western main line from Cardiff General to Newport. At Long Dyke Junction (4), a GWR branch headed south towards Roath Docks (9). Located to the west of the overbridge that carried the ex-Rhymney Railway line from Adam Street (5) to the docks (9) was the GWR's Newtown goods complex. At Tyndall Street (6) there was a complex series of junctions, which provided a link between the Cardiff Railway line towards Bute West Dock (1) and the Rhymney Railway line. The presence of the LMS is relatively limited, being the ex-LNWR Tyndall Street goods yard (10).

The South Wales Railway — later to become part of the

GWR — opened on 18 June 1850. The expansion of the dock facilities saw the construction of the Bute East Docks between 1855 and 1859. The Rhymney Railway's East Dock branch opened in September 1857. The LNWR Tyndall Street branch followed in 1875; the ex-LNWR goods yard closed on 1 July 1933, although it was retained after that date as a siding until the wholesale closure of the various dock lines after nationalisation. Newtown goods yard (8) was originally opened in 1872 and expanded in 1889 and again in 1910. The Cardiff

Railway, supported by the Bute Docks Co as a means of providing additional competition to the existing railways and as a means of circumventing the increasingly fraught industrial relations of the region, was opened on 15 May 1909.

Today, the scene is radically different. Bute East Dock still survives, although casual viewers may not appreciate its once important commercial traffic; the contemporary scene sees the once-bustling dockside now the site of desirable harbourside apartment blocks. The network of lines that once served the docks has completely disappeared, with the exception of the ex-GWR route from Long Dyke Junction, that still provides access to the various freight terminals to the south of the scene, and the ex-GWR main line from Cardiff towards Newport. The latter carries passenger services from three TOCs, First Great Western, Virgin Cross Country and Wales & West; however, with the creation of a proposed new Welsh franchise, local services will pass to a new TOC in the future. The Newtown goods yard passed to National Carriers, but was later to close completely. By the early 1990s the once impressive goods yard was awaiting redevelopment and the building was demolished in the mid-1990s. The ex-RR line south of Adam Street into the docks closed completely on 21 December 1964. (38279/685127)

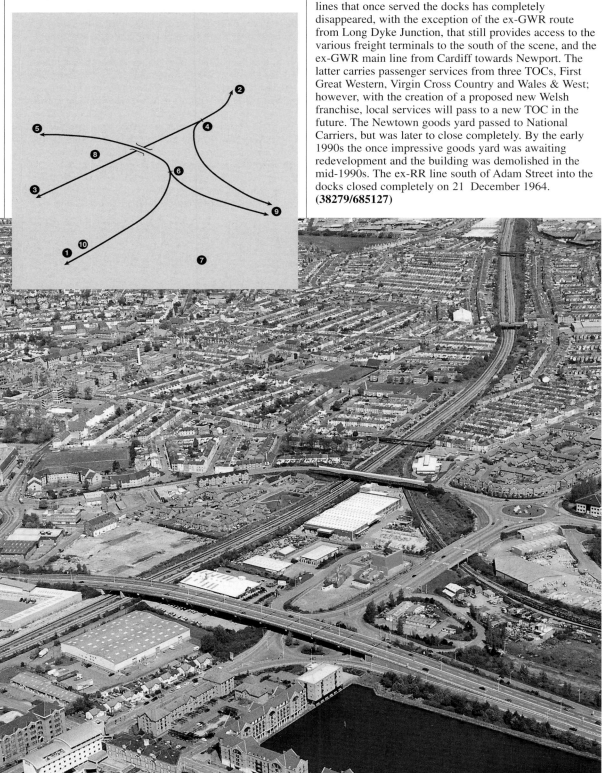

CARNFORTH

Famous as the location where David Lean filmed much of the classic Celia Johnson and Trevor Howard film *Brief Encounter*, Carnforth was and is an important junction on the West Coast main line as this pair of photographs, taken looking west, clearly indicates. Dominating the 'Then' photograph is the ironworks (1), to the east of which the West Coast main line heads north towards Carlisle (4) and south towards Lancaster (5). To the west of the ironworks, there is a triangle of lines formed by Station Junction (10), East Junction (7) and Furness & Midland Junction (8), with lines heading towards Wennington (3), Barrow (9) and Lancaster (5). The Furness Railway platforms of Carnforth station can be seen at the south end of the photograph (6), whilst further to the west can be seen the ex-Furness Railway engine

shed (11); this had already been closed (in 1927 when the LMS transferred work to the ex-LNWR shed further to the south) but would not be demolished until 1941. Also shown is the joint Furness/Midland goods yard (2).

The Lancaster & Carlisle — forerunner of the LNWR — opened the first line through Carnforth, when the section between Lancaster and Kendal was opened on 22 September 1846; initially single track, the route was doubled by December of the same year. The Ulverstone & Lancaster, forerunner of the Furness Railway, opened to freight traffic on 10 August 1857 and to passenger traffic on 26 August of the same year. The joint Midland/Furness line from Wennington opened to F&M Junction for freight on 10 April 1867 and to passenger traffic on 6 June the same year. The curve from East Junction to Station Junction was not opened until 2 August 1880; the rebuilt station at Carnforth was also opened at the same time. Until this date, the trains heading to and from Wennington had their own station at F&M Junction.

The LMSR extended the Furness part of the station in 1940, capacity which proved useful from 3 January 1966 when the services between Leeds and Lancaster were diverted to run via Wennington. However, on 4 May 1970, the platforms on the West Coast main line were taken out of service. Today, the electrified West Coast main line services rush past the site of the redeveloped ironworks, whilst passenger services continue to use the Furness side platforms. Local services are provided by Northern Spirit and First North Western. The site of the Joint Goods yard remains in use whilst adjacent to F&M Junction there are extensive sidings at Bottom End for use by the Civil Engineers. However, the line between F&M Junction and East Junction has now been severed. Although the original FR shed was demolished in 1941, the LMS built a replacement shed on the site in 1944; this was closed on 5 August 1968 and was later to form the basis of the Steamtown railway museum. Although the museum is now closed, the shed remains in use by preservationists, primarily — as can be seen — for the storage and restoration of coaching stock.

(42018/687393)

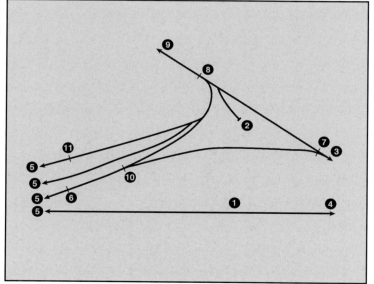

CHEPSTOW

Then: 12 April 1921
Now: 15 March 2000

Situated on the west bank of the River Wye as it enters the Bristol Channel, the town of Chepstow was once, as is clearly shown in the first of these two photographs, an important local centre of shipbuilding with the necessary railway infrastructure to serve the industry. The first railway to serve the town was the Great Western's line from the west which opened on 18 June 1850; the line from the east came later, opening on 19 September 1851. The Brunel-designed bridge, which acted as a template for his future bridge across the Tamar at Saltash, was opened as a single-track structure on 19 July 1852 and doubled in April 1853.

change in the near future. As can be seen, the station remains although it has been reduced to only the two platform faces and the goods facilities have been completely eradicated. Another casualty is the loss of the signalbox visible on the extreme left of the 'Then' photograph. However, the major change at Colwyn Bay is not the diminution of the railway facilities — dramatic though these be — but the construction of the dual carriageway (the A55) between the town and the sea, which passes underneath the approaches to the station in a short tunnel.

(R24111/687395)

CRAVEN ARMS

> *Then: 9 September 1948*
> *Now: 30 April 2000*

Named after a local coaching inn, Craven Arms (& Stokesay) station is situated on the line between Shrewsbury and Hereford. Apart from serving the North & West route, Craven Arms is also the junction for the route towards Swansea — the Central Wales Line — and

was also the point at which the trains from the independent Bishop's Castle Railway terminated until the BCR's closure in April 1935. Further north from the junction with the Bishop's Castle Railway, a second line branched off from the main line, heading northeast towards Much Wenlock. The line, promoted by the sponsors of the Shrewsbury & Chester and engineered by Thomas Brassey (who also took out a lease on the line's operation), opened south from Shrewsbury to Ludlow, via

Craven Arms, on 21 April 1852 as a double-track route. The line from Ludlow to Hereford, which was originally single track, opened to freight on 10 July 1852 and to passenger services on 6 December 1853. The line became jointly controlled by the London & North Western and Great Western Railways in mid-1862, and remained a joint line through the Grouping years. The first section of the Knighton line, forming part of the future Central Wales line, opened on 1 October 1860 for mineral traffic. The station was known as 'Craven Arms' until 1879 when it became 'Craven Arms & Stokesay'; it has now reverted to the shorter name.

The first of these two photographs shows the extensive facilities that existed at Craven Arms shortly after nationalisation in 1948. Apart from the station itself, the six-road LMS carriage shed is situated to the north of the station. South of this is the engine shed. The original shed, built by the Shrewsbury & Hereford Railway, was replaced by the one illustrated here in 1869. Originally

comprising four roads, the shed was reduced by one road in April 1937.

Today Craven Arms remains a junction on the line between Shrewsbury and Hereford. Passenger services are provided by Wales & West over both the main line and over the Central Wales line, although this may well change in the near future as franchises are relet and the possibility of a Welsh franchise is progressed. As can be seen the engine shed has gone — it was closed on 22 May 1964 and later demolished — to be replaced with a housing estate. The station is much diminished, with only platform shelters today, replacing the original station buildings. Reflecting the decline in freight witnessed throughout much of the network, the goods shed and yard have disappeared, with facilities having been withdrawn in 1968. A remarkable survivor, however, is the carriage shed to the north of station seen amongst the weed-strewn sidings that once served it.
(R10092/685135)

DARLINGTON

Then: 1 April 1964
Now: 25 January 2001

There are few more historic railway centres in the British Isles than Darlington, nominal western terminus of that pioneering line from Stockton to Darlington that opened in 1825. Taken looking northwestwards, this pair of photographs records the scene immediately to the north of the town's main station, Bank Top. In the 'Then' photograph it is possible to see clearly the level crossing that existed at this point between the East Coast main line running north towards Newcastle (2) and south towards York (1) with the line between Darlington North Road station (9) and Stockton (3). In the distance, the line can be seen heading towards Bishop Auckland (4) with a

second line heading westwards towards Barnard Castle (5). From Hopetown Junction (11), there is a short freight spur whilst to the north of the line at North Road is the massive ex-North Eastern Railway Darlington Works (10). From Albert Hill Junction (7) to Parkgate Junction (6) one of four spurs provides a direct link between Bank Top and North Road stations. In the foreground is the original locomotive shed of the Great North of England Railway (8) which dated to the early 1840s.

The Stockton & Darlington Railway opened on 27 September 1825 from Witton Park, four miles west of Bishop Auckland, through Darlington to Stockton. The S&DR then constructed the route southwards toward The Croft from Albert Hill Junction; this section opened on 27 October 1829 but it was subsequently acquired by the Great North of England Railway, which opened its line from York to Darlington on 30 April 1841 to passenger services and to freight on 4 April the same year. The line was extended north from Darlington, thereby creating the level crossing, on 15 April 1844 for freight and 19 June 1844 for passenger services. The route westwards from Darlington to Barnard Castle and thence via Stainmore over the Pennines) opened from Darlington 8 July 1856. North Road station was largely rebuilt in 1842 and the structure remains largely unchanged today. Both the GNoER and the S&DR were to become parts of the North Eastern Railway. Darlington Works was initially constructed by the S&DR and opened in 1863; however, in July of that year, the NER took over the S&DR. In October 1864 the works constructed its first locomotive and gradually it replaced Gateshead as the NER's primary locomotive works. Steam locomotive construction continued through until 1957, when BR Standard No 84029 emerged. Diesel locomotive construction continued until 1964 when Type 2 (Class 25) No D7597 was completed. By the time that the 'Then' photograph was taken, the works was already operating on borrowed time. It was to close completely on 2 April 1966.

Today, the course of the original S&DR from Albert Hill Junction through North Road station towards Bishop Auckland remains and sees a regular passenger service courtesy of Northern Spirit. East of Albert Hill Junction, however, the original S&D line has closed — traffic ceased over the section between Albert Hill Junction and Lingfield Lane on 21 May 1967 — although the site of the crossing and of its associated curves is still clearly visible. The East Coast main line — now electrified — remains as does the original locomotive shed of the GNoER — a truly remarkable survival. Not so fortunate, however, is the former locomotive works; its site has been cleared and redeveloped. At North Road station Hopetown Junction is still extant, providing access into the railway museum established at North Road. The branch from Parkgate Junction towards Bishop Auckland has now been singled, although North Road station itself retains a loop. **(A124514/687557)**

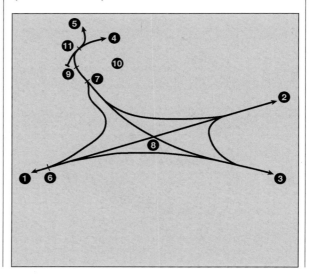

DUMFRIES

Then: 28 June 1973
Now: 11 January 2001

Situated on the Glasgow & South Western main line, Dumfries was an important junction, with the G&SWR route heading westwards towards Castle Douglas and a Caledonian Railway branch heading eastwards to connect with the West Coast main line at Lockerbie. Slightly north of the town, at Cairn Valley Junction, the shortlived G&SWR branch to Moniaive headed northwestwards. This pair of views illustrates the changes to have affected this Scottish town over the past quarter century.

In the first view, the G&SWR main line can be seen heading south towards Carlisle (1) and north towards Glasgow (2) through Dumfries station (3). In the

foreground (4) can be seen the ex-G&SWR goods yard — there was another slightly to the north of the station which was ex-CR — whilst in the background it is possible to identify the remains of the line towards Castle Douglas (6) and towards Castle Douglas Branch Junction (5), where it connected to the G&SWR main line.

It was on 16 July 1846 that the Glasgow, Dumfries & Carlisle Railway was authorised. The first section of the company's line to reach Dumfries, that from Gretna in the south, opened to a temporary station on 23 August 1848; initially the line was worked by the Glasgow, Paisley, Kilmarnock & Ayr Railway. With the opening of the line from Dumfries to Closeburn on 23 October 1849, the station was relocated; this station was itself to be replaced in 1859 by the construction of the station illustrated here. The relocation of the station was in connection with the opening of the line Castle Douglas on 7 November 1859. The CR route from Lockerbie was opened on 1 September 1863. The last expansion of the local network occurred on 1 March 1905 when the Cairn Valley Light Railway opened. By the date of the 'Then' photograph, much of this local network had already been closed. The line to Moniaive lost its passenger services on 3 May 1943 and closed completely on 4 July 1949. The line between Lockerbie and Dumfries lost its passenger services on 19 May 1952 and closed completely on 18 April 1966. Finally, the line towards Castle Douglas lost its passenger services on 14 June 1965, at which point the line west of Maxwelltown — slightly to the west of Dumfries — closed completely. Thus, at the time of the 'Then' photograph, the line towards Castle Douglas was freight-only.

Today, Dumfries retains its services on the alternative route from Glasgow to Carlisle, with passenger services operated by ScotRail. As can be seen, although there is still limited freight handled on the site of the goods yard, the majority of the site has been redeveloped. The passenger station itself survives with its platform canopies. The Maxwelltown branch, which was mothballed at the time of the 'Now' photograph is shortly to receive major investment and be reopened for freight traffic.
(261268/687407)

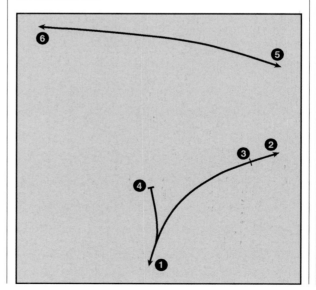

DUNFERMLINE

Then: 18 March 1966
Now: 12 January 2001

Famous for its abbey (7), Dunfermline was at the centre of a complex of railway lines, all built by the North British Railway as shown in this pair of photographs taken looking northwestwards. In the 'Then'

photograph, the relative positions of the town's two stations are clearly shown, with Dunfermline Lower (1) in the foreground on the line between Edinburgh (2) and Cowdenbeath (3) with Dunfermline Upper (4) to the north on the line between Cowdenbeath (5) and Alloa (6). Also visible in the distance is the single-track line (8) that ran further north to join the Cowdenbeath-Perth line at Kelty.

The first of these lines to serve Dunfermline was that from Thornton Junction, which opened to Crossgates, west of Cowdenbeath, on 4 September 1848 and thence to Oakley (on the route towards Alloa), via Dunfermline, on 13 December 1849. The line through Dunfermline Lower opened on 1 November 1877, with a branch heading towards Culross from Charlestown Junction (slightly to the west of the town), on 1 July 1906. The single-track railway towards Kelty had its origins partly in one of the many wagonways established in the Dunfermline area to exploit the local mineral wealth — the Elgin Railway — which had been built to a 4ft gauge in the late 18th century. This network, which included a branch to Dunfermline, opened in 1834, was gradually to lose its importance as the standard gauge network expanded and much was to subsumed within the new West of Fife Mineral Railway which opened in 1858. The connection with the Dunfermline-Stirling line was added in 1866 and between 1894 and 1926 a passenger service operated over the line.

The decline in the Fife coalfield has led to a great reduction in the railway infrastructure in this part of Fife. Today, only the line through Dunfermline Lower remains open for passenger services, with the original line towards Oakley, Alloa and Stirling closed completely. Passenger services over the route ceased on 7 October 1968 and the line closed completely through Dunfermline on 10 October 1979. However, the line to Culross and on to Kincardine remains open from Charlestown Junction. As can be seen, the contemporary scene at Dunfermline shows the curve of the surviving line with a rebuilt

Dunfermline station. A new dual carriageway heads past the station towards the site of the former Dunfermline Upper, which has now been redeveloped. To the west of the town it is still possible to identify the line of the former route towards Stirling. A second station in Dunfermline — Dunfermline Queen Margaret — was opened in 2000, although this not illustrated.
(A159814/687416)

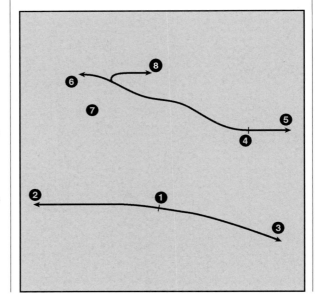

DURHAM

Then: 29 April 1966
Now: 12 January 2001

Although the station and viaduct illustrated here dated
from the late 1850s, it was not until some 15 years later
that this location's importance increased with the opening
of two deviations to the East Coat main line, which

resulted in ECML services running through Durham. The
viewpoint is towards the north, with the city's prominent
cathedral and castle off the frame towards the east. At the
centre of the photograph is the viaduct, which opened to
freight traffic between Auckland Junction (on the
Leamside route to the northeast of Durham) and Bishop
Auckland on 19 August 1856. The line — and station at
Durham — opened to passenger services on the following

1 April. It was not until 1868 that the line northwards from Newton Hall Junction towards Gateshead was opened. The final link — from Reilly Mill Junction to the Leamside route towards Ferryhill at Tursdale Junction — was not opened until 1 October 1871. At that time, ECML services were diverted to run through Durham.

This station was not the first built to serve the city. The first, constructed under the auspices of the Durham & Sunderland Railway, had been built to the northeast at Sherburn House; this opened on 6 November 1837. It would be extended further into Durham with the opening of the line to Durham Elvet in 1893. A second station, Durham Gilesgate, was opened further north on 15 April 1844, but this was to lose its passenger services in 1857 on the opening of the line illustrated here to passenger services. It remained, however, as a freight yard until complete closure on 7 November 1966. Passenger services were withdrawn from Elvet on 1 January 1931.

Today, Durham continues to see passenger services, which are now operated by a number of Train Operating Companies. The main ECML services are handled by

Great North Eastern, whilst additional long distance services are operated by Virgin Cross-Country. Local services are currently operated by Northern Spirit, although proposals for a revised trans-Pennine franchise may well see this changed in the near future. The original line towards Bishop Auckland — indeed all the lines that used to deviate from the ECML at Reilly Mill Junction — has closed whilst to the east, the old ECML via Leamside has been reduced to freight use only. The ECML is now electrified and, in the 'Now' photograph, a northbound Great North Eastern Railway service can be seen entering the station. Further north, a loco-hauled mail train can be seen heading southwards. Durham station retains its platform canopies, although these have been refurbished and modified in the light of the loss of the bay platforms at the north and south end of the station. The signalbox, located at the south end of the Down platform in the earlier view has also disappeared as has the water column at the south end of the Up platform.
(A160856/687422)

Then: 26 May 1954
Now: 24 April 2000

Located at the heart of the Cambridgeshire Fens and the home of one of the most dramatic of all English cathedrals, Ely is an important junction situated on the ex-Great Eastern main line between Cambridge and King's Lynn. North of the station (beyond the views illustrated here), aided by the avoiding line, the ex-GER lines to Peterborough and Norwich head off westwards and eastwards respectively. To the south, further ex-GER routes headed eastwards to Bury St Edmunds and westwards to St Ives. With the exception of the line to St Ives, all these routes remain operational.

The railway first reached Ely courtesy of the Eastern Counties, which opened its route from Newport (south of Cambridge) to Brandon on the Norwich line on 30 July 1845. This was followed by the opening of the lines to Peterborough (on 10 December 1846 to freight and on 14 January 1847 to passengers), King's Lynn (on 26 October 1847), Sutton (on 16 April 1866; extended to St Ives on 10 May 1878) and Bury St Edmunds on 1 September 1879. Passenger services over the line to St Ives were withdrawn on 2 February 1931, although the line remained open for freight to Sutton until 13 July 1964. The main station building dates back to the original building constructed for the Eastern Counties Railway.

Today, Ely remains an important junction and, as can be seen, the station is remarkably unchanged in almost half a century. The platform canopies, though rebuilt, have survived the introduction of electric services — on 22 August 1992 — although the goods yard has disappeared. Passenger services are today operated by a number of Train Operating Companies: West Anglia Great Northern provides EMU services between King's Lynn and London; Anglia Railways provides a cross country link between Ipswich and Peterborough; and Central Trains provides a cross country link from Birmingham to Norwich or Stansted Airport.
(R20617/685140)

FALMOUTH

Then: 16 August 1947
Now: 15 March 2000

Railways reached the Cornish town of Falmouth courtesy of an extension of the broad gauge line from Truro which opened on 24 August 1863. As is evident in the first of these two photographs, Falmouth possessed — as it still does — an extensive harbour; indeed the Fal estuary represents one of the best natural harbours in the British Isles although its commercial traffic declined in favour of ship repairing from the late 19th century. This activity is clearly evident in the 1947 photograph with three vessels in dry dock. The terminus at Falmouth was located to

facilitate a connection with the docks that were under construction at the same time. This connection opened in 1864.

Today, the terminus at Falmouth Docks has been reduced to that of a single track. Indeed, for a short period in the early 1970s, passenger services ceased to operate into the station illustrated here. On 7 December 1970, a new station, half a mile closer to Truro was opened and the existing Falmouth station was closed. However, this closure was reversed when services were reinstated to Falmouth Docks on 5 May 1975. Alongside the passenger station, the busy port of Falmouth retains its rail link, although at the time of writing this is not in regular use. There are proposals, which have existed for a number of years, for the considerable expansion of Falmouth as a container port; if these do progress then the railway will see a dramatic increase in freight traffic, but there is no time scale for this development.
(R9232/684293)

FELIXSTOWE

Then: 9 February 1952
Now: 24 April 2000

The dramatic 'Then' view of Felixstowe Beach station shows the damage caused to the adjacent caravan site as a result of flooding in early 1952. The disastrous East Coast floods of 1952 occurred as a result of a combination of high tides and gale force winds on 31 January 1952. The floods that resulted caused much loss of life and considerable disruption through much of East Anglia.

The initial railway serving Felixstowe was built by the Felixstowe Railway & Pier Co and was opened on 1 May 1877. Operation of the line was taken over by the Great Eastern Railway on 1 September 1879 and the railway was acquired by the GER in 1887. On 1 July 1898 the

GER opened a deviation from Trimley to a new terminus at Felixstowe Town with the result that services to Felixstowe Beach and Felixstowe pier now had to reverse in the new terminus. Already by the date of the 'Then' photograph passenger services had ceased between Beach and Pier stations (on 2 July 1951).

Although now closed, Felixstowe Beach station remains largely intact. Freight facilities were withdrawn from Felixstowe Beach in December 1966. Passenger services between Town and Beach stations were withdrawn on 11 September 1967, but this closure has been more than compensated for the by the dramatic growth of freight traffic through Felixstowe harbour, which is now one of the most important container terminals in Britain. In order to deal with the growth in freight, the original alignment from Trimley along the north bank of the Orwell estuary was reopened on 13 May 1970 whilst the south-west curve at Felixstowe Town was also reinstated to facilitate freight traffic. The south-east curve at Felixstowe Town, over which passenger services had operated until 1967, was closed on 27 April 1970. Reflecting the importance of container traffic to the port, a Freightliner terminal was opened at Felixstowe on 28 November 1972. Situated to the east of Beach station there is still a caravan park between the railway and the sea. **(A48297/685147)**

GAINSBOROUGH

Then: 4 July 1939
Now: 19 April 2000

The Lincolnshire town of Gainsborough was, and is, an important junction serving the lines between Scunthorpe, Lincoln, Retford and Doncaster. This pair of photographs concentrates on one of the town's stations — Central (1) — which is located on the line towards Barnetby (2). At Trent East Junction (4), this line meets the line from Lincoln (3), which serves the town's second station — Lea Road. Having crossed the River Trent, the line reaches Trent West Junction (7), where one route heads

west towards Retford (5) and the other north towards Doncaster (6).

The first railway to serve Gainsborough was the Great Northern route from Lincoln, which opened on 9 April 1849. This was followed by the Manchester, Sheffield & Lincolnshire Railway — later part of the Great Central — which opened its line from Grimsby to Gainsborough on 2 April 1850 and extended this route through to Retford and Sheffield on 16 April 1850. Stuck at the end of a GNR branch, most of Gainsborough's traffic was routed via the MS&LR line, with the result that the GNR line to the town was mothballed for three years prior to the completion of the company's link to Doncaster, which

opened on 15 July 1867. The GNR route from Doncaster through Gainsborough to Lincoln was to be transferred to the Great Northern & Great Eastern Joint, when this was established in 1888.

Although much of rural Lincolnshire lost its railway services in the post-Beeching era, Gainsborough has survived remarkably unchanged, with all four lines still carrying passenger services, although the lightly-used and poorly-served line between the town and Scunthorpe has been under some threat in recent years. It still, however, carries passenger services and these, therefore, continue to serve Central station. The station itself, however, has fared less well, with the facilities on offer much reduced; gone are the substantial buildings of 1939. In 1939, there was evidence of substantial freight traffic at Central; this too is now but history, with the line now reduced to double track through the station only. A curious survival, however, revealed in the slightly wider angle offered by the 'Now' photograph is in the foreground on the east side of the line opposite the site of the now-demolished goods shed. This structure is the old MS&LR single-track engine shed; out of use by 1899, its survival more than 100 years after it last housed a locomotive is surprising.

(62188/685156)

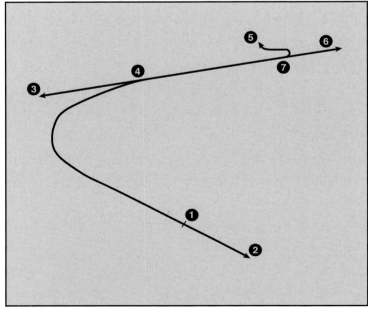

GATESHEAD

Then: 7 August 1972
Now: 12 January 2001

Located on the south side of the River Tyne, Gateshead is dominated by its larger neighbour to the north, Newcastle, and this is no more evident than in the position of the railways serving the Tyne. Looking northwestwards, the 'Then' photograph records the scene as it existed in the early 1970s. Immediately south of the High Level Bridge (6) can be seen the platforms of Gateshead West (1) and East (2) stations, whilst in the background the familiar sight of Newcastle Central station (3) is evident with the complex Castle Junction (4) where the East Coast main line heads off towards Berwick and Edinburgh (5). In the foreground, the line heads towards Sunderland (8) past Oakwell Gate Sidings (7). To the west of Newcastle station is West Junction (10) where the line divides between the routes towards Scotswood (11) and Durham (12); the latter meets up with the line (9) from Gateshead West at King Edward Bridge Junction.

Great Eastern branch terminus, is situated off to the east; this branch was completed on 31 October 1843. The Hatfield-Hertford line was opened on 1 March 1858; this provided a connection with the Eastern Counties (Great Eastern) line. The Hertford loop was proposed in the last years of the 19th century as a means of relieving congestion on the East Coast main line and was authorised in 1898. The GNR already possessed a short branch at Alexandra Palace to Enfield (which had opened on 4 April 1871) and the railway obtained powers to construct the new loop. From Grange Park to Cuffley, the line opened on 4 April 1910. A single track from Cuffley to Langley Junction at Stevenage was opened to freight on 4 March 1918 and the second line was completed two years later, being opened to freight on 23 December 1920. Passenger services over the loop were not introduced until 2 June 1924.

The Hertford loop today continues to provide the town with a suburban service between Stevenage and London which is now operated by West Anglia Great Northern. The line is also regularly used by long-distance services diverted from the East Coast main line. The station is largely unchanged although railway facilities have been much diminished with the closure of the line towards Hatfield and the loss of the link towards Hertford East (which is also now served by WAGN EMU services). Even by the date of the 'Then' photograph passenger services had ceased between Hatfield and Hertford North, being withdrawn on 18 June 1951. The line between Hertford North and Hertford East had also closed completely by the date of the 'Then' photograph, succumbing on 9 September 1963, although the track had not been lifted by 1965. The section of line westwards from Hertford North to Attimore Hall Siding closed completely on 23 May 1966. The Hertford loop was electrified with EMU-operated services reaching Hertford North on 8 November 1976, being extended to Stevenage in 1979.
(A148645/685739)

HIGHBRIDGE

Then: 31 May 1968
Now: 15 March 2000

Time was when Highbridge, situated on the Somerset Coast between Bridgwater and Weston-super-Mare, was an important railway intersection with a station possessing seven platform faces — with the ex-GWR section known as 'West' and the ex-S&DJR known as 'East' — as well

the workshops of the Somerset & Dorset Joint Railway. Unfortunately, much of this had already disappeared by the date of the 'Then' photograph, but enough remained in 1968 to give a good impression of the extent of the railway facilities in the town.

The broad-gauge Bristol & Exeter Railway opened between Bristol and Bridgwater on 14 June 1841. This is the line running north-south through both illustrations. On 28 August 1854 the line from

Highbridge Wharf to Glastonbury opened; this crossed the B&ER line on the level and was worked by the B&ER until 1862. It was in 1862 that the Somerset Central Railway — one of the constituents of the Somerset & Dorset — made its appearance and in that year that the first part of Highbridge Works opened. The works, which were situated to the east of the station (and thus off to the right of the photographs), were to close with much loss of labour in 1930. Beyond Highbridge, a 1.75-mile long extension was constructed to Burnham (-on-Sea after 1920). This line was to open on 3 May 1858.

As already intimated, Highbridge was a much reduced railway town by 1968. The Burnham-on-Sea extension had lost its passenger services on 29 October 1951 (except for summer excursions) and was to close completely on 20 May 1963. The line to Highbridge Wharf, along with the connection to the ex-GWR line, was to close completely on 17 May 1965. Passenger services were withdrawn from Evercreech to Highbridge (given the suffix '& Burnham-on-Sea' in 1952 in place of 'East') on 7 March 1966 (at which time the line closed completely

beyond Bason Bridge). Finally, the connection from Highbridge to the United Dairies' siding at Bason Bridge closed completely on 2 October 1972. Apart from the trackbed of the closed line to Highbridge Wharf and Burnham heading westwards, the 'Then' photograph shows well the original station at Highbridge, the remaining section of the ex-S&DJR line heading towards Bason Bridge and the ex-GWR West signalbox that controlled the level crossing at the north end of the station.

Today, Highbridge station is a pale shadow of what existed even 32 years ago. All traces of the S&DJR have now disappeared as have West signalbox and the original station buildings. Another casualty is the goods shed; freight facilities were withdrawn in November 1964 — again prior to the date of the 'Then' photograph although the shed was still extant four years later. Today the ex-GWR main line sees long-distance services provided by First Great Western and Virgin Cross-Country, whilst all local services are currently in the hands of Wales & West.

(A184176/684256)

HUDDERSFIELD

Then: 10 September 1968
Now: 20 May 2000

There are few more dramatic stations architecturally in Britain than that in Huddersfield. The Grade 1 listed station building was started in 1846 to the design of J. P. Pritchett (Junior), who was based in York. Facing St George's Square, the station has a 416ft-long facade with a central portico supported on Corinthian columns. At either end of the facade are secondary structures; these housed the offices and other facilities of the two companies that ran services into Huddersfield — at the north end the building was occupied by the London & North Western and at the south by the Lancashire & Yorkshire. Behind the facade, the station's overall roof

was the result of expansion work undertaken in the 1880s when the viaduct to the north of the station was also extended. Another building of note prominent in St George's Square, on the north side, is the George Hotel; this establishment has one great claim to fame for those interested in sport — it was here in 1895 that the inaugural meeting of the Northern Rugby Union — later the Rugby League — was held.

The first railway to serve Huddersfield was that from Heaton Lodge Junction to the north; this route, eventually to form part of the LNWR's trans-Pennine route between Manchester and Leeds was to open on 3 August 1847. It was not until 1 August 1849 that the line was extended through to Stalybridge. Huddersfield became a junction with the opening of the L&YR's line towards Sheffield on 1 July 1850. The only other pre-Grouping company to serve Huddersfield was the Midland, which possessed a freight-only line, opened on 1 November 1910, to serve the Newton goods depot. This depot was located northwest of the passenger station and was to close in August 1968.

The 'Then' photograph shows well the station and its

immediate environment at about the time Huddersfield Council took over responsibility for the historic station. Thirty years on, the station has been cleaned and the trainshed restored. Today, the booking office is located in the central block of the facade, whilst the southern half of the main building, including the old L&YR offices, have been converted for use as a pub. Although the ex-MR presence in the town has long gone, the station still sees passenger services over both the ex-LNWR route between Leeds and Manchester and over the ex-L&YR route towards Penistone. The summer timetable in 2000 saw a further improvement to local passenger links, with the reopening of two curves between Huddersfield and Halifax thus facilitating the restoration of passenger services between Huddersfield and Bradford. Currently, local passenger services are provided by First North Western and Northern Spirit, although with the planned redistribution of franchises in the area and the creation of a dedicated trans-Pennine franchise, this will probably change in the near future.
(24369/685691)

INVERNESS

Then: 30 July 1963
Now: 11 January 2001

Inverness represented the focal point of the Highland Railway's activities and the scale of the company's legacy to the town is evident even 40 years after it ceased to be an independent company. This pair of views, taken looking southeastwards across the River Ness, provide a graphic indication of how much this part of Inverness was dominated by the railways. In the 'Then' photograph, the town's railway station (1) is accessed from the lines towards Perth (4) and Nairn (5) by lines passing through Welsh's Bridge Junction (9), whilst the lines to the Far North (7) approach the station through Rose Street Junction (10). The Perth and Nairn lines diverge at

Millburn Junction (8). Alongside the lines from the south and east is the site of the engine shed (2). This structure was originally opened in September 1863 as a semi-roundhouse and was extended in 1875. In 1933 it was provided by a mechanical coaler and was further altered by BR in the early 1950s. However, the shed closed in June 1961 and was then used for the storage of withdrawn locomotives until August 1962. As can be seen, by the date of the 'Then' photograph, the shed had already been demolished. Also visible in the photograph are Lochgorm Works (3), situated in the triangle to the east of the station, the line serving the Harbour (6) and the extensive freight and carriage sidings provided.

The first section of line to open was that from Inverness towards Nairn, which opened (along with the Harbour branch) on 5 November 1855. This was followed by the line across the River Ness to Invergordon on 25 May 1863. The final phase in the direct railway development of the town came with the opening of the line from Daviot to Inverness on 1 November 1898, thus completing the shorter route southwards towards Perth. Lochgorm Works, which initially included a locomotive running shed until the opening of the roundhouse in 1863, dated to the start of that decade. Many of the most famous of HR locomotive designs emerged from Lochgorm; however, after Grouping, the works gradually lost its status, being regarded as a Subsidiary Locomotive Works and coming under the control of St Rollox in Glasgow.

Today, Inverness is still an important railway location, with passenger services continuing to operate over the Far North lines to Kyle of Lochalsh, Wick and Thurso as well as over the routes towards Perth and Inverness. The majority of passenger services are provided by ScotRail, although Great North Eastern still provides a direct service to London via the line to Perth. There has, however, been some rationalisation, particularly with the singling of the line towards Aberdeen from Welsh's Bridge Junction and the simplification of the approaches

from the east. The branch to the harbour, disused from the late 1980s, has also disappeared, but the buildings of the former workshops remain extant and in use. To the north of the line towards Nairn, there is still considerable freight traffic, with sidings to serve cement terminals, coal yards and an oil terminal. Although the lines to Inverness and beyond have been under threat on several occasions, most recently under the Serpell proposals of the early 1980s, tourism and the oil industry helped to ensure that the lines survived into the 21st century. A threat of a more natural form occurred in 1989 when floodwater caused the bridge across the River Ness to fail; the bridge was, however, rebuilt, although there was considerable disruption to railway services for the period of closure. **(A119504/687433)**

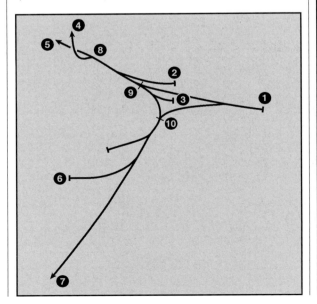

Then: 1949
Now: 30 April 2000

Today, with Abraham Darby's iron bridge as its centrepiece, the Shropshire village of Ironbridge is both a World Heritage site and the destination for many thousands of tourists and visitors, all of whom make their way to see this masterpiece of 18th century engineering and to enjoy the excellent museums on offer through the Ironbridge Gorge Museum Trust. Fifty years ago, however, when the 'Then' photograph was taken, the story was very different. The Shropshire coalfield was in decline and the other staple industries of the region were also gradually disappearing; few tourists visited the region and, indeed, the whole concept of Industrial Archaeology was still to be fostered.

As is evident in the 'Then' photograph, situated on the southern side of the River Severn was the station of Iron Bridge & Broseley. The station was one of the intermediate stations north of Bridgnorth on the Severn Valley line towards Shrewsbury. The Severn Valley line opened on 1 February 1862.

Today, although the trackbed of the line remains extant, there is little evidence of the station. Passenger services between Bewdley and Shrewsbury ceased on 9 September 1963 and the section south from Buildwas to Alveley Sidings closed completely on the following 2 December. Further south, the line from Bridgnorth to Bewdley forms part of the preserved Severn Valley Railway, whilst Ironbridge Power Station is currently served by MGR trains via the line through Coalbrookdale. Over the past four decades the numbers of visitors — as evinced even in April by the number of parked cars — has grown phenomenally. However, an attempt to bring some in by train to a halt at Coalbrookdale was not a conspicuous success. Geologically, the Ironbridge Gorge is relatively unstable and neither of these illustrations shows well how steep the banks are on either side of the river.
(A24217/685166)

KEIGHLEY

Then: 4 April 1968
Now: 20 May 2000

The West Yorkshire town of Keighley is situated in the Aire Valley between Skipton and Bradford. An important industrial community, the town was served by both the Midland and Great Northern railways. This panoramic view, taken looking northwestwards, shows the ex-Midland route stretching towards Skipton parallel to the river with, in the foreground, the junction at Keighley that served both the line between Skipton and Bradford as well as the ex-MR branch to Oxenhope and the ex-GNR line to Queensbury.

The first railway to serve Keighley was the Leeds & Bradford Railway, which opened from Shipley to

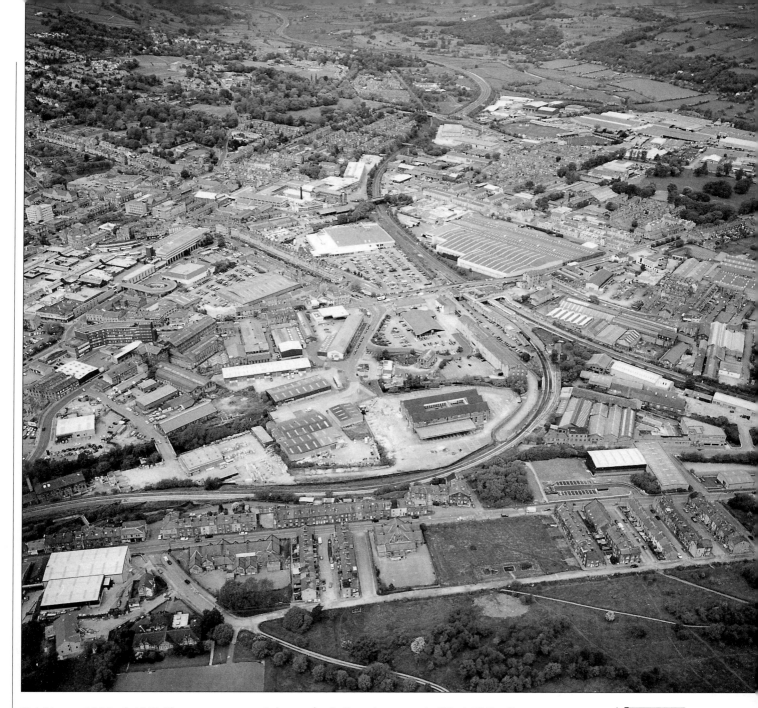

Keighley on 16 March 1847. The route was extended thence to Skipton on 8 September 1847. This line, later incorporated in the Midland Railway and subsequently the LMS, was to form part of the MR's route to Scotland and thus saw regular Anglo-Scottish expresses. Keighley became a junction with the opening of the 4.75-mile branch to Oxenhope, to passengers on 15 April 1867 and to freight on 1 July 1867. The MR dominance of the town was to be threatened with the opening of the GNR line from Ingrow in 1884.

By the date of the first of these two photographs, railway facilities in Keighley had already been significantly reduced. The ex-GNR lines lost their passenger services on 23 May 1955 and the final short section of the ex-GNR route, from Ingrow to the junction with the Worth Valley line, closed on 28 June 1965. Freight facilities were withdrawn from the ex-GNR Keighley South goods yard — accessed via a spur which passed under the Worth Valley line — in 1961. The ex-MR lines had suffered as well, with withdrawal

of all services over the Worth Valley line: passenger services were withdrawn on 1 January 1962 and freight on the following 18 June. This was, however, not to be the end of the story as, shortly after the date of the 'Then' photograph (on 29 June 1968), the Keighley & Worth Valley Railway Preservation Society reopened the line.

Today, Keighley station is still a junction, with the Worth Valley Railway providing regular steam services to Oxenhope and with Northern Spirit providing passenger services. The line as far as Skipton has now been electrified, but DMUs provide a link between Glasgow and Leeds. It is interesting to note that, some 40 years after the building ceased to have a railway function, the ex-GNR goods shed serving Keighley remains standing. The ex-MR goods shed and yard, visible in the 'Then' photograph at the western end of the station are, however, now no more, with the site having been redeveloped into the ubiquitous supermarket and car park.
(A180482/685696)

KESWICK

Then: 7 August 1946
Now: 10 January 2001

Viewed looking northwards, this pair of photographs shows the facilities at Keswick, headquarters of the Cockermouth, Keswick & Penrith Railway. Incorporated on 1 August 1861, the 31.25-mile line was engineered by Thomas Bouch, who also was the engineer of the Stainmore line and the designer of the ill-fated first bridge across the River Tay (for which he was knighted and then disgraced). Although the CK&PR was, to a large extent, dominated by the London & North Western, the Stockton & Darlington (later the North Eastern) Railway held the rights to operate mineral traffic over the route. The line opened to mineral traffic on 26 October 1864 and to passenger traffic on 2 January 1865. Facilities provided included the hotel; this was opened in 1869 and leased to the Keswick Hotel Co, which shared a chairman with the CK&PR.

Today, although the hotel remains open, the railway has closed. DMU operation over the line was introduced on 3 January 1955; along with this initiative, summer Sunday services were also reintroduced and the previously closed halt at Blencow was reopened. The optimism generated by these improvements was, however, soon to be dissipated as the harsh economic realities of the late 1950s impinged. Through freight services were withdrawn on 1 June 1964

— at which time Keswick lost its freight facilities — and passenger services west of Keswick were withdrawn on 18 April 1966. This resulted in the complete closure of the line west of Keswick and services now limited to a DMU service between Keswick and Penrith. Although the then Minister of Transport had refused to sanction closure east of Keswick, BR continued to reduce facilities on the line. All the remaining stations, including Keswick, were reduced to unstaffed halts from 1 July 1968. The final nail in the coffin came with the withdrawal of the last passenger services on 6 March 1972. Today, the hotel is still extant as are the station buildings and platform canopies on the southern platform. The island platform and buildings have been demolished. Further to the east, the bridge over the River Greta shows the alignment of the former railway as it heads towards Penrith. As with a number of other lines recorded in this book, there are tentative proposals for the partial reopening of this line in order to relieve congestion in the northern part of the Lake District; whether anything will come of these, only time will tell.

(**R8046/687442**)

KILMARNOCK

Then: 5 April 1968
Now: 11 January 2001

Kilmarnock in Ayrshire was and is famous as the home of the locomotive builders, Andrew Barclay. It was also an important junction for the Glasgow & South Western Railway with routes radiating out towards Glasgow, the

Ayrshire Coast and Carlisle. In the first of these two photographs, Kilmarnock station (1) is seen at the centre with the GSWR main line towards Carlisle heading eastwards (2). Westwards from the station, it was possible to travel to Glasgow via two different routes: the joint Caledonian/GSW Glasgow, Barrhead & Kilmarnock line heads north (3) towards Lugtown while the GSWR line proper heads west towards Dalry (4). Heading southwest

is the GSWR line towards Barassie (5), whilst also visible are the ex-GB&KJR (6) and GSWR (7) goods yards.

The first railway to serve Kilmarnock was the Kilmarnock & Troon, which was authorised on 27 May 1808 and opened from St Marnocks at Kilmarnock, which was located slightly to the south of the station illustrated here, to Troon via Barassie on 6 July 1812; the Kilmarnock & Troon was bought by the GSWR in 1899. The next arrival was the Glasgow, Paisley, Kilmarnock & Ayr Railway, which opened its line from Dalry on 4 April 1843. The line eastwards towards Auchinleck opened on 9 August 1848. The second route to Glasgow opened on 26 June 1873 when the GB&KJR opened its line from Stewarton.

Today, Kilmarnock remains an important junction, with passenger services running over the ex-GSWR main line to the east, over the ex-GB&KJR to the north and over the ex-GSWR line to Troon. However, the last-named line was to lose its local services on 3 March 1969 and, until 5 May 1975 when it was used for diverted services from the south to Stranraer, it was freight only. Passenger services between Kilmarnock and Irvine ceased on 6 April 1964 whilst local services over the GB&KJR ceased on 7 November 1966. The line from Dalry to Kilmarnock — the original GPK&AR line from Glasgow — lost its passenger services on 22 October 1973 and closed completely on that date. The ex-GB&KJR Hill Street goods yard closed on 30 September 1969.

The contemporary view shows that the passenger station retains it buildings and platform canopies on the northbound platform, although there has been some

reduction of facilities on the southbound. Although the line towards Dalry has closed completely, it is still possible to identify precisely its trackbed. Whilst the ex-G&SWR goods yard has now closed, the site has been redeveloped for use by the locomotive builders Andrew Barclay, whose premises can be seen between the station and the line curving towards Troon.
(A179685/687454)

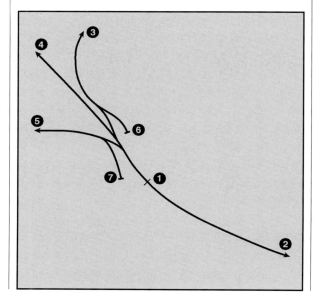

LICHFIELD

Then: 11 May 1972
Now: 19 April 2000

Lichfield possesses two stations: Trent Valley, which is situated on the West Coast main line between Tamworth and Colwich Junction (and thus some distance from the city itself), and City. This pair of photographs illustrates the latter. The first shows the station as it was in the early 1970s looking towards the northeast. The station's two signalboxes are clearly visible as are the numerous semaphore signals that controlled the station. Stabled adjacent to the redundant goods shed — general freight facilities were withdrawn from the station in 1968 — is a rake of seven DMU vehicles representing the stock then in use on the route to Birmingham.

The route through Lichfield City formed part of the South Staffordshire Railway (later London & North Western) route from Walsall to Wichnor, which opened on 9 April 1849. The station became a junction when the line from Sutton Coldfield (authorised on 29 June 1850) opened three and a half years later. The original South Staffordshire Railway station was located slightly to the east of the location illustrated here until July 1871. By the date of the 'Then' photograph passenger services had already been withdrawn from the original route from Walsall to Burton on Trent in 1965, although the line remained open for freight both north and west of City station. At this time passenger services from Birmingham New Street terminated at Lichfield City.

The contemporary shot shows that the station at Lichfield City remains largely unchanged, although both

signalboxes have become the victims of modernisation. The redundant goods shed is also still extant, whilst the coal yard on the east side of the line has disappeared. Gone also are the DMUs; the line has been electrified. The line was integrated with the service southwards from New Street as the Cross-City route; initially launched from Four Oaks in May 1978, the service was extended to run from Lichfield City. From 28 November 1988 Cross-City services were extended north from City to Trent Valley station, thus reopening a short section of the line closed to passenger services in 1965. Electrification of the line was approved in 1990 with a budget of £64.5 million, the sum including some £4.5 million for the resignalling of the line between Aston and Lichfield. Electric services north to Lichfield commenced in November 1992 **(A229773/685291)**

LIVERPOOL

Then: 25 June 1955
Now: 25 January 2001

The City of Liverpool was provided with three major passenger termini, all of which are clearly visible in the first of these views looking southwards in the mid-1950s. In the foreground, however, the route of the elevated Liverpool Overhead Railway (1) can be clearly seen heading south towards Dingle (2) and north towards Seaforth (3). The most obvious of the three termini is the ex-Lancashire & Yorkshire Railway Exchange station (4) with its lines heading north towards Southport and Wigan

(5). To the east can be seen the ex-London & North Western terminus of Lime Street (6) with its lines towards Crewe and Manchester (7). Finally, there is the ex-Cheshire Lines Committee Central (8) with its route heading southwards to Manchester (9). Also visible are some of the great public and ecclesiastical buildings for which Liverpool is famous, such as St George's Hall (10) and the partially constructed Anglican cathedral (11). It would be another 25 years before the latter was completed, by which time the city had also acquired a Catholic cathedral (which is visible in the 'Now' photograph).

The first of the three termini to open was Lime Street,

which was originally opened by the Liverpool & Manchester Railway on 15 August 1836. The original station, designed by John Cunningham, was demolished for the second phase of the station, built between 1846 and 1851 and designed by Sir William Tite. The station was again rebuilt, between 1867 and 1871, with a trainshed designed by William Baker. The work was concluded by the construction of the hotel in front of the trainshed in 1871; this was designed by Alfred Waterhouse and replaced the bulk of Tite's earlier work. Lime Street was followed by the opening of the L&YR/East Lancashire Railway terminus at Exchange on 13 May 1850, when services were diverted from the earlier Great Howard Street. The new station was initially known as Tithebarn Street when opened and the first structure was designed by John Hawkshaw. The high-pitched roofs visible in the 'Then' photograph were the result of rebuilding in 1886-1888. Adjacent to the station was Exchange Hotel, constructed in 1884. The final entrant was the CLC whose Central station opened on 1 March 1874. This station was designed by Sir John Fowler. The LOR opened in four phases between 1893 and 1905; the section illustrated in the 'Then' photograph being part of the first section to open on 6 March 1893.

Of the three termini illustrated in the 1955 photograph, only one, Lime Street, remains operational in the form portrayed some 45 years ago; indeed, the station was undergoing renovation during the period of this volume's compilation. The major change, which is not visible here, is the electrification of the route southwards to Crewe. Both the Central and Exchange stations shown on the 1955 view have closed, the former on 17 April 1972 and the latter on 30 April 1977 although the former is now

served by a new underground station, opened on 3 January 1978, linked into the electrified Merseyrail network. The site of Exchange station has been completely cleared and has been partially used for car parking. The original Central station has also been demolished. Another casualty is the Liverpool Overhead Railway; the so-called 'Dockers' Umbrella' was not to survive much beyond the date of the 'Then' photograph, closing on 30 December 1956 and being demolished the following September despite efforts to reopen it. **(A59817/687568)**

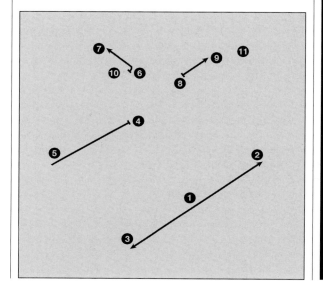

LLANDUDNO

Then: 29 August 1946
Now: 13 January 2001

The coming of the railway to the North Wales coast — as elsewhere in the British Isles — was a stimulus to the growth of tourist traffic to the seaside and many of the Welsh resorts familiar to us today had their origins with the railway boom of the 1840s. One of the places to experience rapid growth in the second half of the 19th century was Llandudno, although the settlement was initially bypassed by the construction of the Chester & Holyhead Railway, which ran some three miles to the south. Whilst the C&HR opened between Chester and Bangor to passenger services on 1 May 1848 and to freight on the following 1 June, it was to be some years before Llandudno itself received a railway connection. Although a railway was authorised in August 1853 to link a proposed harbour to the railway, this was not to progress, although the pier was constructed. The line from a new junction station (opened 1860) to Llandudno was opened on 1 October 1858 and leased to the LNWR in 1862. Following the take-over of the line by the LNWR in July 1873, the branch was doubled and, in 1885, the branch terminus was extended with additional platforms and sidings. The station as illustrated here was the result of a further rebuilding, opening at Easter 1892. With the Orme forming a backdrop, the size of Llandudno — and of its railway station — immediately after World War 2 is apparent in the earlier of these two photographs.

Llandudno retains its railway connection, although the facilities provided are much more basic than those considered essential 50 years ago. The LNWR roof was demolished during the 1990s and the number of platforms in use has also declined from five after the 1892 rebuilding to three today. Gone also are the extensive carriage sidings — no longer required when all services are in the hands of DMUs operated by First North Western. As with other lines in Wales, the proposed creation of a Welsh franchise will lead to further revisions to the route in the future. Today, however, as can be seen, passengers using the station are provided with only the remnants of the once extensive roof at the concourse end of the station. In the 'Now' photograph a two-car DMU of First North Western can be seen awaiting departure. One feature that does survive from the scene 55 years ago is the ex-LNWR signalbox; this 34-lever frame box was constructed in 1891.
(R7568/687460)

LONDON BRIDGE

Then: 9 July 1950
Now: 27 June 2000

It is only from the air that the scale of a station like that at London Bridge can be fully appreciated. This pair of photographs shows the changes that have occurred at this location over exactly 50 years. In many respects, the railway is surprisingly unchanged — although the eagle-eyed will spot many alterations of detail — and it is the surrounding area that has undergone the most radical redevelopment. In the 1950s photograph, evidence of wartime damage is all too apparent with the shells of certain buildings — including, in the background, the trainshed at London Cannon Street (see pages 120/1) —

as is the scale of maritime activity on the south bank of the river. The latter has, by 2000, long disappeared and much of the warehousing and ancillary infrastructure that once served the docks has also largely disappeared. Moored in place of the commercial traffic the docks of London once saw, is the museum vessel, HMS *Belfast*. Also discernible in the 1950 photograph is evidence of the surviving London tramway network; reprieved by the war, by 1950 plans for the complete abandonment of the trams were well advanced — Operation Tramaway — and the last traditional trams would operate in London in July 1952.

Dominating the centre of both photographs is London Bridge station. First opened in mid-December 1836 by the London & Greenwich Railway, it is London Bridge that

can claim to be the first of all London's terminal stations. The L&GR was joined in serving the station by the London & Croydon (later part of the London, Brighton & South Coast Railway) and the South Eastern Railway (which later built its own terminus at Bricklayers Arms (see pages 44/5). In order to accommodate the increased usage, the station was expanded in 1842 and again in 1864 when the through lines to Charing Cross were opened. London Bridge was a joint — in name but not in actions — station controlled by the SER and LBSCR, although competition meant that there was a wall — not breached until the creation of the SR in 1923 — between the two companies' sections. The approaches to London Bridge were widened twice — in 1866 and 1880 — to cater for the growth of traffic. Also constructed at the station was a hotel, although by the date of the 'Then' photograph, this had already been converted to offices and largely destroyed during the war.

The 'Now' photograph shows London Bridge station as it was rebuilt during the late 1970s. The revamped station concourse area was opened by the then Bishop of Southwark, Mervyn Stockwood, on 25 December 1978.

This scheme, which cost some £9 million, resulted in the construction of a new concourse and the removal of the remaining barriers between the LBSCR and SER sections of the station. Prior to the rebuilding of the station, another £21 million had been spent on track modifications and the opening of a new power signalbox — visible in the 'Now' photograph at the country end of the terminal platforms — which was designed to control some 150 miles of track.

Today, all passenger services through and to London Bridge are currently operated by the two Connex franchises and Thameslink, although Connex South Central has not had its franchise renewed and will be replaced sometime during 2001. It has also been announced that Railtrack, as the freeholders of London Bridge station, have plans for the complete redevelopment of the station. This will result in the demolition of the existing trainsheds and the construction of office and retail accommodation on a concrete raft above the track; this work, however, has yet to be approved and, in the meantime, the existing station will remain. **(R13401C/685978)**

LONDON CANNON STREET

Then: 30 August 1929
Now: 27 June 2000

One of a number of London termini that served the
Southern Region and its antecedents, Cannon Street
owes its origins to the South Eastern Railway, which
opened the station on 1 September 1866. The station was
built on a viaduct some 700ft in length; which required
some 27m bricks for its construction. The station facade
was represented by a five-storey hotel designed by E. M.
Barry. This was originally known as the City Terminus
Hotel but was renamed Cannon Street Hotel in 1879.
The roof of the hotel can be seen in the 'Then'
photograph behind the dramatic trainshed, designed by
Sir John Hackshaw, of the station itself. The 'Then'

photograph was taken in 1929, shortly after the introduction of suburban electrification had led to the wholesale remodelling of track at Cannon Street. This had taken place between 5 June and 28 June 1926 and had involved the temporary closure of the station for the duration. Also clearly visible in this view are the approach lines to Cannon Street from Charing Cross and London Bridge, whilst east of the station it is also possible to identify the trainshed of Fenchurch Street station.

The changes wrought on this part of London are dramatic; a whole new cityscape has developed on the north bank of the Thames and Cannon Street station has not been immune from these changes. Much of the reconstruction was the result of rebuilding following wartime damage but the boom in the City has led to wholesale redevelopment over the past 20 years. The only identifiable features of the 1866 station are the towers at the southernmost end of the station and part of the retaining walls. The station was severely damaged by wartime bombing; the hotel (which, by that time had been converted to offices) was to close permanently as a result of Blitz damage in 1941 and the trainshed was also to suffer severely and be subsequently demolished. The area occupied by the station hotel was cleared in the 1960s and new office accommodation built; subsequently this has been expanded by the construction of further office space above the platforms. The track layout was again heavily modernised between 2 August and 9 September 1974 when control of some 150 miles of track was passed to the new London Bridge panel box. Today, Cannon Street is exclusively the preserve of EMUs operated by Connex South Eastern.

(P28617/685988)

which quickly disappear into tunnel again as they head towards Baker Street. The scale of the Great Central's goods yard and shed is apparent on the down side, whilst on the upside can be seen the carriage sheds; these were later to be converted for use as the depot servicing the DMUs used on the suburban services. Although Marylebone itself did not have an immediately adjacent locomotive shed, limited facilities were provided, including a turntable; the 'Then' photograph antedates the construction in the 1930s by the LNER of a mechanical coaler and the turntable provided at the opening of the line is hidden by the goods shed. At the extreme top of the photograph can be seen the trainshed of Marylebone station and, beyond it, part of the Great Central hotel. Designed by Sir R. W. Edis, this was opened in 1899 but was destined to have a relatively short life as a hotel under railway ownership, being converted to offices in 1945. The building served as the headquarters of British Railways from 1948 until its sale in 1986.

Although the angle here is slightly different, it is hard to spot any part of the railway network. The eagle-eyed will, however, be able to make out part of Marylebone station in the middle distance, although the actual station has seen a reduction in the number of platforms and the loss of part of the trainshed. Lord's Cricket Ground in the foreground remains a point of reference, but the once extensive goods yard is no more. This was reduced to coal depot only on 28 April 1952 and was to close completely on 28 March 1966. Marylebone station's importance was significantly diminished on 5 September 1966 when through services over the Great Central main line north of Aylesbury ceased. This meant that the station handled only suburban services to, inter alia, Aylesbury and Banbury. For a period in the 1980s even these were threatened with the line into Marylebone being considered as an ideal route for experimental 'bustitution'. In the event, conventional railway services survived and, with the Chiltern Railway's franchise having recently been extended, the station can look forward to its second century with an expanding network of services operating into it.

(9093/685980)

Then: 12 October 1950
Now: 27 June 2000

There is a curious symmetry between these two photographs taken some 50 years apart showing the southern approaches to London Victoria station. In the 'Then' photograph, Battersea Power Station is under construction, with three of its four chimneys already at work, whilst in the 'Now' photograph, the shell of the old power station stands forlornly, its roof and one side wall demolished whilst a final decision is awaited on its future use. Since the power station closed in the 1980s, there have been a number of proposals for the reuse of this Giles Gilbert Scott-designed building but, unlike the same architect's Bankside Power Station (now converted into Tate Modern), Battersea gradually deteriorates.

The comparison of these two views shows that the railway infrastructure in this locality is largely unchanged. The freight yards on the south bank of the Thames have been closed — Battersea Wharf lost its freight facilities on 4 May 1970 — the carriage sheds on the north bank of the river are still extant as part of the train shed at Victoria station, although the Brighton side of the station has been rafted over and a shopping complex built over the platforms.

The origins of the station and of the approaches across the river date to the 1850s when the London, Chatham & Dover and London, Brighton & South Coast railways jointly promoted the Victoria Station & Pimlico Railway, which was incorporated in 1858. Although the relationship was never wholly harmonious, the station grew to become one of the largest serving London. The LBSCR platforms were opened on 1 October 1860; these were used by the LCDR from 3 December 1860 until its own platforms were opened on 25 August 1862. As the GWR had running powers into the station — indeed was a part owner of the station until 1932 — some of the LCDR track was dual gauge in order to accommodate the GWR's broad gauge trains from Southall. The station was considerably expanded prior to World War 1, the LBSCR section being completed in 1908 and the SECR — as the LCDR had become — in 1909. It was only with the creation of the Southern Railway in 1923 that the division of Victoria into two stations with separate stationmasters ceased.

Today, the successors of the LBSCR and SECR — Connex South Central and Connex South Eastern — currently provide the majority of passenger services, although the station is also the terminus for the highly profitable Gatwick Express franchise for passenger to and from Gatwick Airport.
(**A33462/686003**)

LONGPORT

Then: 7 September 1962
Now: 30 April 2000

Although catalogued by Aerofilms as Newcastle under Lyme, this location is actually Longport, to the north of Stoke on Trent, on the ex-North Staffordshire Railway line towards Kidsgrove. Viewed looking northwards, the 1967 photographs shows clearly Longport station, with its two platforms, the freight depot on the east side of the line, the sidings on the west side of the line and the junction, just to the north of the station, for the branch that linked this line with the North Staffordshire loop line through Tunstall. Beyond the junction there is a brief four-track section heading northwards to Chatterley.

Surveyed by George Stephenson, work started on the construction of the NSR in 1846. The sections from Stoke, through Longport, to Crewe and from Harecastle (later Kidsgrove) to Congleton opened on 5 October 1848. The branch — called the Tunstall Lower Branch (or the Pinnox branch after the exchange sidings serving the collieries of the Chatterley-Whitfield Colliery Co) — was authorised on 25 July 1864, although its usefulness was to diminish when the Loop line was eventually opened. It remained a minerals-only line throughout its existence. It is interesting to note that, although the Tunstall branch had closed completely prior to the date of the 'Then photograph (on 17 February 1964), it was still intact at its westernmost end, being used to gain access to the covered freight depot.

Today, although the scene looks remarkably unchanged in many ways — the station is still extant and both the freight depot and down sidings remain — closer examination reveals that much has happened in the past 33 years. Most obvious is the construction of the A527 road to the west of the railway and running parallel with it. To the south of the station, the level crossing has now been abolished, whilst the line has also been electrified at 25kV as part of the West Coast main line scheme. Electric services through Stoke on Trent commenced on 5 December 1966. Ironically, the NSR had itself obtained powers to electrify the route in 1904, building a power station at Chatterley to that effect. In the event, electrification of the railway did not proceed and the power generated was used to haul barges through Harecastle canal tunnel.
(A106834/685306)

LUTON

Then: 1931
Now: 20 May 2000

Viewed looking northwards, this pair of photographs shows the changes wrought at the north end of Luton over the past 70 years. Dominating the scene in the earlier of the two photographs is the ex-Midland Railway goods shed; notice running behind it one of the small open-top tramcars operated by Luton Corporation. By 1931, the electric trams were coming to the end of their life in the Bedfordshire town, the last operating in service on 16 April 1932. The ex-MR main line runs from west to east through Luton, whilst in the foreground can be seen the ex-Great Northern Railway route heading west from

Luton (Bute Street) towards Dunstable, with the goods shed prominent in the foreground.

Although Luton came to rely upon the ex-MR route, it was the future GNR line that was the first to serve the town. Opened on 3 May 1858, the line to Dunstable provided a link to the LNWR main line at Leighton Buzzard and it was the LNWR that operated the line until 1 September 1860 when the GNR opened its line eastwards towards Welwyn. The MR main line was to open for freight between Bedford and London St Pancras on 8 September 1867 and to passenger services to Moorgate on 13 July 1868. Passenger services into St Pancras commenced on 1 October 1868. The scene illustrated in the 'Then' shot records the ex-MR station in the years just prior to its rebuilding in 1937-1940. Also

visible in the photograph is evidence of the locomotive servicing facilities provided by both the MR and GNR. The small turntable located at the west end of the station represented the MR's facilities whilst west of the GNR goods shed on the northern side of the line is the site of the GNR shed. The GNR shed closed about 1901 when most of the structure was demolished; the remains of the building were used as a store until October 1970 when it was demolished completely.

At the time the 'Then' photograph was taken passenger services operated throughout over the ex-GNR line; however, these were to be the first casualties, being withdrawn between Dunstable and Hatfield on 26 April 1965 (the section between Dunstable and Leighton Buzzard had ceased on 2 July 1962). In 1966 a connection was installed to the south of the two stations allowing freight services to access the Dunstable line from the ex-MR route, thus allowing the ex-GNR line east from Luton to close completely on 3 January 1966. Today, although the branch towards Dunstable as been mothballed (since 30 April 1989), the connection has been severed. As can be seen, both the former goods yards have been closed — freight facilities being withdrawn in the 1960s — and the impressive sheds demolished; the GNR yard has been converted to provide car parking for passengers. The hipped structure at the west end of the station, however, remains. The line was electrified in 1983. Today, long distance services are provided through Luton by Midland Main Line whilst local services are operated by Thameslink.
(35122/685701)

Then: 17 June 1938
Now: 30 April 2000

Famous during the Industrial Revolution as one of the major centres of the silk trade, Macclesfield in Cheshire is located some dozen miles south of Stockport. This pair of views, taken looking south, shows the approaches from the north to Macclesfield Central station. In the earlier of the two photographs, recorded just before the outbreak of World War 2, the main line runs from north to south; a short three-coach train has just cleared the junction and is heading north towards Stockport. At the junction, the joint LMS/LNER line heads northeastwards towards Marple, whilst in the foreground is part of the LMS goods yard.

Despite its importance as an industrial centre, Macclesfield was destined to be bypassed by the first phase of the Manchester & Birmingham Railway; it was to be linked to the M&BR via a branch constructed from Cheadle (Cheadle Hulme from 1866) that opened on 24 November 1845. At Macclesfield, the M&BR (later LNWR) route eventually made an end on connection with the NSR route from Congleton, but this could be achieved until the completion of the short tunnel to the north of Hibel Road station. The North Staffordshire line from Congleton to Macclesfield opened to passenger services on 13 June 1849 and to freight on the following 18 June. The Macclesfield, Bollington & Marple Railway,

authorised in 1864, was jointly promoted by the North Staffordshire and Manchester, Sheffield & Lincolnshire (later GC) railways, and opened on 2 August 1869 for passenger services and to freight on 1 March 1870. The MB&MR possessed its own terminus in the town until the opening of Central station on 1 July 1873; the old MB&MR station remained as a freight terminal until closure in September 1969. Central was, however, the town's lesser station; the primary station was at Hibel Road — slightly to the north of the scene illustrated here.

Today, Macclesfield Central is the town's only station and has lost the 'Central' suffix. Macclesfield Hibel Road closed on 7 November 1960 and the original Central station was rebuilt in connection with the 25kV electrification of the West Coast main line and its branches. Electric services started to operate through Macclesfield in two stages: north to Cheadle Hulme on 14 June 1965 and south to Congleton on 5 December 1966. The Macclesfield-Rose Hill line was a relatively late passenger closure, with services being withdrawn on 5 January 1970, at which time the line was to close completely. As can be seen, today there is virtually no trace of the erstwhile MB&MR route; the trackbed has been used to provide part of the route of an improved A523. Another casualty has been the old LMS goods yard in the foreground, although this site has yet to be fully redeveloped.
(57634/685170)

Then: 11 May 1959
Now: 16 April 2000

Sitting astride the River Medway, Maidstone possesses today three passenger stations, two of which are visible in this set of views taken looking northeastwards. In the foreground is Maidstone West station (1), which is situated on the line between Paddock Wood (2) and Maidstone Barracks and Strood (3). The second route to serve the town is that from Swanley (4) running through Maidstone East station (5) and the 358yd-long Wheeler Street Tunnel (6) before heading off towards Ashford (7).

Although all the lines that serve Maidstone passed from the South Eastern & Chatham Railway in 1923 to the Southern Railway, the origins of the two routes lay in the earlier constituents of the SECR — the South Eastern and the London, Chatham & Dover railways. The first of the railways to serve Maidstone was the SER which opened its branch from Paddock Wood to Maidstone on 25 September 1844 and was extended northwards to Strood on 18 June 1856. This was followed by the line from Otford to Maidstone East, which opened under the auspices of the Sevenoaks Railway on 1 June 1874 and was extended to Ashford on 1 July 1884, having become part of the LC&DR in 1879.

Today, both the routes through Maidstone remain and now form part of the Connex South Eastern franchise. In the foreground, Maidstone West's facilities have

undergone some modification. However, whilst the passenger services remain, Maidstone's freight facilities have completely disappeared, with those at East succumbing in 1965. The freight yard at West has been completely redeveloped.
(A75254/684520)

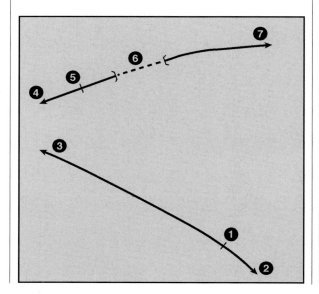

MALDON (ESSEX)

Then: Pre-World War 2
Now: 16 April 2000

Whilst Braintree was at the northern end of the Maldon, Witham & Braintree Railway and still sees passenger services, Maldon was the terminus at the southern end and is now wholly without railway connections. The line opened from the junction at Witham (on the London-Colchester main line) to freight on 15 August 1848 and to passenger services on the following 2 October. The railway constructed a remarkable station — later called Maldon East and from 1889 Maldon East & Heybridge — as its southern terminus. Built in a superb Jacobean style, the structure was the result of local politics. Prior to the construction of the railway, the line was taken over by the Eastern Counties Railway, whose deputy chairman, David Waddington, was ambitious politically and was seeking

election from the Maldon constituency. The employment of a large number of construction workers at the station was, it has been suggested, a factor in Waddington's successful election.

A second line serving Maldon was opened on 1 October 1889; this left the Southminster line at Woodham Ferrers and served a second station, called Maldon West, before making a junction with the existing line just to the northwest of the terminus illustrated in this view

The 'Then' photograph records Maldon East & Heybridge prior to World War 2. The branch to Woodham Ferrers was to lose its passenger services on 10 September 1939, although through freight was to continue for a further 14 years and on 1 April 1953 freight services were withdrawn from the section west of Maldon West; this station was then served as a spur from Maldon East until 1 September 1954 when

Visible in the first of these two photographs, viewed looking east, in the foreground is the earlier Elizabeth Dock (1) with the extensive railway network serving them. There is also a link towards the Senhouse Dock (2). This section of line was originally owned by the Maryport & Carlisle Railway. The Dock branch can be seen curving towards the main Cumbrian Coast line, heading towards Carlisle (3) and Barrow (4). The ex-Maryport & Carlisle station (5) is to the north of the junction, whilst to the south is the ex-M&CR goods shed (6). Slightly to the south of this point, the M&CR made an end-on junction with the London & North Western Railway (7).

The Maryport & Carlisle Railway was authorised on 12 July 1837, with the first section, from Maryport northwards opened on 15 July 1840. Initially built as single track, the line north from Maryport was doubled in the late 1840s. A further Act, of 26 June 1855, authorised the construction of a new station — with a single 1,000ft-long platform and closer to the town — which was to open on 4 June 1860. This is the station, built in red sandstone, that is illustrated in the 'Then' photograph. The site also included the headquarters of the M&CR, but these had been demolished in 1960. Also authorised by the 1855 Act was the construction of the Elizabeth Dock and the M&CR branch to serve it; these opened in 1857. The line had already been extended south of Maryport under the auspices of the Whitehaven Junction Railway by the date of the station's move; the line from Maryport to Workington opened on 19 January 1846. Initially this line was operated by the M&CR, but control (and operation) was eventually to pass to the LNWR.

Today, Maryport is but a pale shadow of its earlier form. The railway is now restricted to serving the Cumbrian Coast route alone, with passenger services currently provided by First North Western, and all rail connections to the docks have now disappeared. The decline in the town's railway facilities is an accurate reflection of the more general decline in the region's heavy industry that has resulted in virtually the complete elimination of the local iron and steel trade. The impressive station itself is another casualty, being demolished in the early 1970s and replaced with more basic facilities. As can be seen, all the lines that were once provided here for the shipment of mineral traffic have been removed, although it is still possible to identify the route in part. Reflecting the changing fortunes of the locality, the once busy commercial harbour area has in part been landscaped and part of the land used for housing. The Cumbrian Coast line, however, does survive and two other notable survivals are the ex-M&CR goods shed (6), albeit no longer in railway use, and the LMS-built signalbox of 1933 (8), which was upgraded slightly in 1979 by the addition of a panel in addition to its original lever-frame.
(A130559/687461)

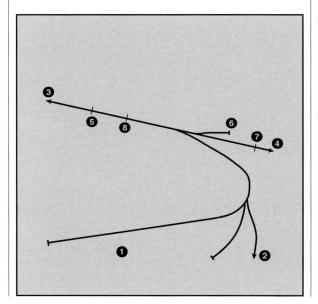

MELROSE

Then: 25 November 1950
Now: 12 January 2001

The borders' town of Melrose is famous as the site of one of the great ruined abbeys of the British Isles. The ruins of the abbey are clearly visible in the first of these two photographs; the foreground is, however, dominated by the town's railway station.

Melrose was one of the intermediate stations on the North British Railway's main line from Edinburgh to Carlisle, a line known as the 'Waverley Route' after the novels of Sir Walter Scott (one of the most famous of local residents). The line opened from a junction with the Edinburgh & Dalkeith Railway at Dalhousie through Melrose and St Boswells to Hawick on 1 November 1849. Although it had always been the company's intentions to extend southwards to Carlisle — thus opening an

alternative route for Anglo-Scottish services — it was not until the 1860s that the NBR's plans came to fruition. The Border Union Railway — from Hawick to Carlisle — opened throughout on 1 July 1862. Initially, the NBR was dissatisfied with results of the BUR and it was not until 1876, with the opening of the Settle & Carlisle line and the inauguration of through services to London over the Midland Railway route, that fortunes improved.

At the time the earlier of these two photographs was taken, the Waverley route still represented an important link in the railway network. However, nationalisation and the worsening of the railway industry's financial position highlighted the number of Anglo-Scottish routes with the result that the Waverley route became threatened. Melrose lost its freight facilities in 1964 and loss of passenger services was foreshadowed in the Beeching Report. Despite a vigorous campaign to retain the route — including disruption of the final service over the route — Melrose and the rest of the Waverley route was to close completely on 6 January 1969. An ambitious preservation

scheme for the route failed, unfortunately, to secure the line and BR seemed desirous of eradicating the route as quickly as possible. A decade later, Melrose was largely untouched, but this was soon to change as a new road made use of the trackbed through the station.

Today, the new road can be seen cutting a swathe across the landscape, utilising the route of the erstwhile Waverley route (including the location of the road bridge) in bypassing the town centre. The construction of this road may well have scuppered any prospect of the reopening of the Waverley route throughout, although judging by the amount of traffic visible on it perhaps the good Dr Beeching ought to be allocating a celestial closure notice for it. In terms of railway infrastructure, the main station buildings on the eastbound platform have been preserved and found alternative uses, including acting as a restaurant. The eastbound platform also survives; however, on the westbound side of the station, the new road has completely obliterated all traces. **(A34320/687467)**

MILES PLATTING

Then: 12 July 1964
Now: 30 April 2000

Located to the northeast of Manchester Victoria station, Miles Platting is the junction between the line from Manchester to Rochdale with that heading towards Ashton under Lyne. At the south end of the triangle, Miles Platting station served both the Manchester-Rochdale and Manchester-Ashton lines. In the distance can be seen the Manchester Loop, which provides an alternative route from Manchester Victoria northwards and meets the Rochdale line at Thorpes Bridge Junction. On the north side of the station are Tank Yard Sidings, these and the associated Brewer marshalling yard are linked to the Oldham Road goods depot that is served by a branch

heading southwards slightly to the west of Miles Platting station (and just out of view in this photograph).

The first railway to run through Miles Platting was the Manchester & Leeds Railway (later the Lancashire & Yorkshire), which opened from its terminus at Oldham Road on 4 July 1839 to Littleborough. Passenger services continued to serve Oldham Road until 1 January 1844 when the line to Hunts Bank (Victoria) was opened as was the new station at Miles Platting. The branch to Ashton opened on 13 April 1846; this line was promoted by the Ashton, Stalybridge & Liverpool Junction Railway. It, like the Manchester & Leeds, was later to become part of the LYR. The Loop line, which was intended to provide additional capacity between Thorpes Bridge Junction and Victoria, opened in 1877.

Today, the triangular junction at Miles Platting remains, although with the closure of the goods depot at Oldham

Road and the more general decline in freight traffic on the railways the sidings to the north of the station have disappeared. There is, however, evidence still of some limited freight traffic, with the presence of a Tilcon stone terminal on the south side of the line. The vast area of slum clearance seen in the 1964 photograph has seen some new housing but the residential area in the foreground recorded in 1964 has been swept away and replaced by commercial redevelopment. The track has been heavily rationalised and the station has been closed and demolished. Services today through the site of the former station continue to operate on both the Rochdale and Ashton lines and are in the hands, currently, of First North Western and Northern Spirit. Also still extant is the Loop line, although this is used primarily for freight and diversions.

(A136881/685180)

MILLERHILL

Then: 6 April 1960
Now: 12 January 2001

It is frightening to contemplate with this pair of photographs both the scale of the new marshalling yard at Millerhill then under construction alongside the sheer waste that this facility represented once the death-knell was sounded for both wagon-load freight and the Waverley route on which it was located. When announced, the Millerhill marshalling yard was portrayed as one of the three most important investments under the 1955 Modernisation Plan for freight in Scotland alongside similar developments at Perth and at Thornton (Fife). The

new yard was designed to replace the existing yards at Niddrie and Portobello and provide a link with the Kingmoor yard at Carlisle.

The line through Millerhill owed its origins to the Edinburgh & Dalkeith Railway which was built to the gauge of 4ft 6in and was opened in 1831. The line was bought by the North British Railway in October 1845 and in 1846 the track was regauged to standard gauge. It was reopened, after regauging, to freight on 7 July 1847 and to passenger traffic on 14 July 1847. The reason for the NBR's interest in the line was the fact that, on 31 July 1845 the NBR had been authorised to construct a line from South Esk, on the E&DR, to Hawick. This route, opened progressively between 1847 and 1849, was to form part of the NBR's ultimate scheme for constructing a line through to Carlisle — the Waverley route — that was finally to be completed in June 1862. At the time of the construction of the Millerhill yard, the Waverley route was still perceived as an important route for freight traffic as well as still carrying passenger traffic. The scale of the yard was also a reflection of the fact that the Lothian coal field was still active and that the British Transport Commission believed in the future of wagon-load freight. Another factor was the opening of a car factory at Bathgate and the expected flow of components between the West Midlands and the new plant and of finished vehicles from it.

However, the new yard was a white elephant almost from the moment that it was completed in 1962/63. A change of emphasis at the highest level saw containerisation as offering a future for freight as the economics of wagon-load continued to deteriorate. It was decided that Edinburgh's container terminal would be established at Portobello. A more serious impediment to the future of the yard came with the decision to close the Waverley route, all traffic ceasing on 6 January 1969, although the northern stub serving Millerhill yard was retained. The yard's importance vanished overnight, although it remained to serve the remnants of the local coal industry, such as the collieries at Bilston Glen and Monktonhall.

Today, although the Waverley route south of the yard has disappeared, along with the track forming the western half of the yard, that on the east largely remains and, as can be seen, is well used although it can only be accessed from the south. To the south of the yard the line towards the East Coast main line at Monkton Hall Junction heads to the east whilst adjacent to the wagon works a second line heads southwards towards Millerhill Junction. Whilst the Waverley route at this point is but a pale shadow of its former self, there are proposals — albeit long term — for the possible reopening of the line southwards to Hawick.

(R38407/687476)

MILL HILL

Then: 1924
Now: 22 May 2000

Evidence of the northwards expansion of London is all too apparent in these two photographs of Mill Hill taken three-quarters of a century apart. The first, taken shortly after the London, Midland & Scottish Railway had been

created, shows the ex-Midland Railway station with the four-track main line heading northwards. In the foreground, and passing under the ex-MR main line, is the ex-Great Northern Railway (by 1924 LNER) route to Edgware. At the time this photograph was taken the ex-GNR station was known as The Hale (for Mill Hill); it was renamed Mill Hill (for The Hale) on 1 March 1928. The Great Northern Railway line towards Edgware opened

on 22 August 1867. This meant that the GNR reached Mill Hill slightly earlier than the MR, whose route southwards from Bedford to St Pancras opened for freight on 8 September 1867 and for passenger services to Moorgate on 13 July 1868. Passenger services started to serve St Pancras on 1 October 1868. The 1924 photograph illustrates well the traditional Midland Railway station with the platform canopies.

In the contemporary illustration, two things are immediately evident: the vast expansion in the number of houses, with suburbia stretching well out into the countryside, and the construction of the M1 motorway parallel to the railway line. In terms of railway facilities, the four-track main line survives, with passenger services now provided by Midland Main Line (long distance) and Thameslink (suburban), and has been electrified. Suburban services between Bedford and St Pancras were electrified

in 1983. However, the station has been much reduced in terms of platform accommodation and the small goods yard has closed (in August 1964). The ex-MR station acquired the suffix 'Broadway' in 1950. The major casualty has been the disappearance of the ex-GNR line. Passenger services were withdrawn between Edgware and Finchley on 11 September 1939 as part of the proposals to integrate and electrify the ex-GNR 'Northern Heights' services as part of the expanded London Transport Underground network. In the event, the section from Mill Hill East to Finchley reopened on 18 May 1941 but the remainder of the route was not so treated. Freight continued to operate west of Mill Hill East to Edgware until complete closure west of Mill Hill East on 4 May 1964. As can be seen, the rail overbridge to the south of Broadway station has disappeared and the cutting has been infilled. **(10721/685709)**

MOUNTAIN ASH

152

> *Then: 1932*
> *Now: 1 May 2000*

Reflecting the competition to exploit the mineral wealth of the Welsh valleys in the 19th century, the close proximity of the two routes serving the Aberdare Valley of the Cynon River is self-evident in the first of these two views, taken looking northwards, of Mountain Ash. The Aberdare Valley was fought over by the Great Western and Taff Vale railways and both stations can be seen in the 'Then' photograph. In the background is the GWR Cardiff Road station (6) situated on the line between Quakers yard (1) and Aberdare (4), whilst in the foreground is the ex-TVR Oxford Street station (5) situated on the route between Abercynon (2) and Aberdare (3). Running between the two competing lines is a mineral line (7), that provided the only physical link between the two routes at this point.

The first railway to serve the valley was the Aberdare Railway, which was authorised on 31 July 1845 to construct an eight-mile line linking Aberdare with the TVR at Navigation House (called Abercynon from 1896). Freight services over the route were introduced in July 1846 and passenger services commenced on 6 August the same year. Initially built as single track, the route was doubled a decade later. The Aberdare Railway was leased by the TVR from 1 January 1847 and fully absorbed on 31 July 1902. The second route — the Vale of Neath — was authorised on 3 August 1846 and opened to passenger services on 24 September 1851 and to freight in the following December. The Vale of Neath was initially constructed as a broad-gauge line, but become mixed gauge in the early 1860s. A connecting line (8 to 9) was opened in 1864 but was disconnected in 1913.

By the date of the 'Then' photograph all the lines here had become part of the enlarged GWR; but it was not until

after Nationalisation that major rationalisation took effect. The first casualty was the passenger service over the ex-TVR route, withdrawn on 16 March 1964, although it was to be reinstated on 2 October 1987. Also withdrawn in 1964, on 15 June, were passenger services on the ex-GWR route through Cardiff Road station. The section of the ex-GWR route from Cardiff Road southwards to Cresselley Crossing closed completely on 1 March 1965, and that northwards to Aberdare (High Level) on 29 November 1971 with the section between Middle Duffryn and Mountain Ash being transferred to the NCB.

Today, passenger services continue to operate to Aberdare through Mountain Ash, with services provided by Cardiff Railway Co, over the route which was singled on 20 October 1968. There is still some limited coal traffic, emanating from the last deep pit in the Valleys — Tower at Hirwaun — but all evidence of the once thriving coal industry at Mountain Ash has disappeared. Of the former GWR line, there is also now little evidence, although the road over bridge to the north of Cardiff Road station provides a reference point. Since the 'Now' photograph was taken, the station has been slightly relocated and a loop installed.

(40012/685184)

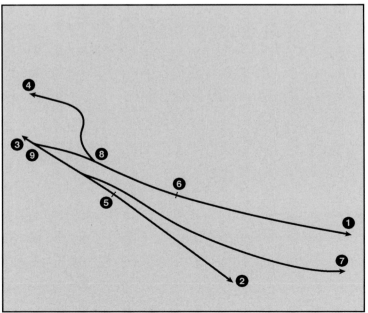

being operated by Sealink. Although suffering from poor facilities and difficult tidal conditions, Newhaven was an early target for the railways. Under the aegis of the Brighton, Lewes & Hastings Railway, the six-mile branch from Southerham Junction at Lewes opened to Newhaven (Town) on 8 December 1847 and the cross-Channel services previously operated from Shoreham — and from 1867 under the control of the railway company — transferred to Newhaven. Newhaven Harbour station opened on 17 May 1886. The branch to Seaford opened on 1 June 1864. The Seaford branch was originally built as single track but was doubled in 1905 and it is shown as double track in the first photograph. In the centre of the photograph can be seen the platforms of Newhaven Harbour station, with Newhaven Marine in the foreground. Further north it is possible to identify Newhaven Town station. From Newhaven Harbour Junction, the branch heads eastwards to Bishopstone and Seaford.

In the contemporary photograph, one of today's generation of ferries reverses into its berth at Newhaven at the end of its crossing from Dieppe. Rail access to Newhaven Marine remains, although it is effectively out of use. Elsewhere, the railways at Newhaven have been largely reduced to a passenger only service from Lewes to Seaford, operated (currently) by Connex South Central. The sidings and associated facilities between Town and Harbour stations have largely disappeared although some buildings remain to give reference points. **(A127610/684528)**

NEWQUAY

Then: 27 May 1961
Now: 15 March 2000

The Cornish coast has long proved a popular holiday destination and numerous resorts have sprung up to serve the many thousands that visit the region annually. One of the most popular of destinations is Newquay. The railway reached Newquay, under the auspices of the Cornwall Minerals Railway's route from Fowey, in the mid-1870s; it opened for freight on 1 June 1874 and to passenger services on 20 June 1876. From the following year the line was leased by the GWR and finally taken over by that company in 1896. A second GWR line serving Newquay — from Chacewater via Perranporth — opened on 2 January 1905. The junction with the Newquay-Fowey

line was at Tolcarn Junction, which can just be identified in the distance. The length of the platforms give some indication of the level of traffic expected, particularly in the summer months, whilst the signalbox at the platform end was relocated there in early 1946. Also situated beyond the platform end was a small two-road engine shed, but this had long gone even by the date of the earlier photograph, having been demolished in 1936.

Forty years after the date of the earlier photograph, Newquay retains a passenger service to Par. Although the original platforms are intact, there is evidence that the platform canopies have been cut back and the station remodelled. Freight facilities were withdrawn

from Newquay on 7 September 1964 and, today, the site of the former goods yard is occupied by a retailer. Although not visible in the 'Now' photograph, Tolcarn Junction no longer exists as the line towards Perranporth lost its passenger services on 4 February 1963 and was to close completely between Tolcarn Junction and Trevemper Line Siding on 28 October the same year. Today, the bulk of services are in the hands of Wales & West, with the occasional long-distance service from First Great Western and Virgin Cross-Country on summer Saturdays.
(A90119/684287)

NEWTON ABBOT

Then: 11 July 1972
Now: 15 March 2000

Viewed looking south, the extent of the railway station and former railway workshops at Newton Abbot is evident in these photographs. Although the 'Then' photograph was taken as late as the early 1970s, the arrangement at the station — with its two long island platforms — is largely as it was rebuilt by the Great Western Railway (the station being officially reopened on 11 April 1927). On the south side of the station can be seen the diesel depot (NA; earlier 83A). The diesel depot comprised two elements, part of the steam shed — built in 1893 and closed to steam in April 1962 — alongside a modern purpose built diesel depot. A westbound service can be seen in the

station and a second rake of coaches, with a Class 08 shunter, is adjacent in the carriage sidings. Also to the south can be seen the remains of the South Devon Railway workshops.

The South Devon Railway reached Newton Abbot on 30 December 1846 when the line from Teignmouth opened. The line westwards from Newton Abbot to Totnes opened on 20 July 1848. Initially services were locomotive-hauled, using locomotives hired from the GWR, but from 10 January 1848 the section between Teignmouth and Newton Abbot was converted to run atmospherically. The system was never a great success and was abandoned later in 1848. Although the line westwards from Newton Abbot to Totnes was built with the atmospheric system in mind, it was never used west of Newton Abbot. The South Devon Railway branch from Aller Junction, just to the west of the station, to Paignton and Kingswear opened on 18 December 1848. The line from Newton Abbot northwards towards Moretonhampstead, promoted by the Moretonhampstead & South Devon Railway, opened on 4 July 1866. The South Devon Railway was worked by the Great Western

Railway from 1 February 1876 and two years later the SDR ceased to exist as a separate company.

Today, Newton Abbot remains an important junction, although facilities have been much reduced. Resignalling in the late 1980s resulted in the replacement of the semaphore signalling and the disappearance of the old boxes at the east and west end of the station. The number of platforms in use has also diminished, with services now concentrated on the southernmost of the island platforms. The station building, however, and the platform canopies remain from the scene 30 years ago. The shell of the former steam shed, roofless since the 1970s, stand alongside the derelict diesel depot; with the introduction of InterCity 125s in the mid-1970s the need for a locomotive depot at Newton Abbot disappeared and the shed closed in the early 1980s. Passenger services continue to pass through Newton Abbot on the ex-GWR main line between Exeter and Plymouth and over the line to Torquay and Paignton. Although the Moretonhampstead line has largely disappeared, there remains a freight link northwards from Newton Abbot to Heathfield.
(A235883/684329)

NORTHALLERTON

Then: 14 April 1972
Now: 12 January 2001

Located between York and Darlington, Northallerton is one of the most important junctions on the East Coast main line, providing a link with Tees-side via the line towards Yarm. This pair of views, taking looking southwards, shows to good effect the complex junctions here. At the centre of the 'Then' photograph is

Northallerton station (1), with the ECML heading southwards to York (2). Heading southwestwards (3) can be seen the already closed line towards Ripon, which joined the ECML at Cordio Junction (9). Until closure, the Ripon line could access both the Northallerton-Yarm line and the ECML at this point, but with closure the arrangement had been simplified. ECML-Yarm traffic could be routed via Longlands Junction (7) and Boroughbridge Road Junction (8) to avoid the station. To the north the ECML heads towards Darlington (4) whilst

the Wensleydale line towards Redmire heads off to the west (5). Finally, the two lines towards Yarm (6) meet up to the east of the photograph at Northallerton East Junction.

The first line to serve Northallerton was the Great North of England Railway which opened between York and Darlington for freight traffic on 4 January 1841 and to passenger traffic on 30 March 1841; a station was provided at Northallerton from the start. The Leeds & Thirsk line, from Melmerby to Stockton, opened on 2 June 1856. There was no physical connection at Northallerton until the curve from the station towards Stockton on 1 January 1856. Thereafter, until the route was doubled in 1901, the section between Northallerton and Melmerby became less important. The connection between the Melmerby line and the ECML was also constructed in 1901. Also at this time the Longlands Junction (down)-Boroughbridge Road Junction section was added. The Boroughbridge Road Junction-Longlands Junction (up) section was not built until the 1930s. Although passenger services over the line to Redmire had ceased by the date of the 'Then' photograph (on 26 April 1954), the line remained open for freight traffic. The line towards Ripon lost its passenger services on 6 March 1967 and at the same time was to close completely between Cordio Junction and Melmerby.

Today, Northallerton retains its station on the ECML as well as the complex junction serving the line towards Yarm. Also still extant, although the junction arrangement has been altered, is the line towards Redmire; although this route did close briefly, it was restored for use by the military in the late 1990s. As can be seen, the complex junctions at Northallerton remain, although the junction to

the line towards Redmire has been severed; this route is now accessed by a curve running west-north slightly out of the frame. Also readily apparent is the increased size of the town, with housing stretching much further south than was the case 30 years ago. In the foreground a three-car DMU operated by Northern Spirit heads southwards along the East Coast main line towards the station. In the distance it is possible to identify the station at Northallerton; this has been rebuilt, although the platforms remain staggered. **(A225534/687583)**

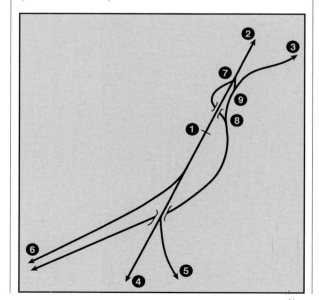

taken over by the CR, whose enthusiasm for the newly-approved line was not great. It was not until 1 June 1870 that the line opened from Callander to Killin, and from there to Tyndrum, the line opened in August 1873. It was not until 1 April 1877 that the line was further extended — to Dalmally — and the final extension to Oban was opened on 30 June 1880.

As can be seen in the first of these two views, taken in 1959, the facilities provided by the railway at Oban were extensive, with a large station, with overall roof, carriage sidings and freight facilities. There was also an engine shed located slightly inland; this was to be closed in 1963. Today, Oban is still an important railway destination, although its services no long travel the full length of the Callander & Oban line. In 1897 a connection was made at

Crianlarich between the C&O route and the North British line to Fort William. From 1 November 1965 the line eastwards of the connection at Crianlarich (with the exception of a short spur for loading timber) was closed completely, with all services being diverted over the ex-NBR route. As can be seen, although the station at Oban remains in the same location, the attractive building constructed by the Callander & Oban Railway is no more, being demolished in the mid-1980s when planning permission was granted for the construction of a supermarket on part of the site. As is also clearly evident, there has been considerable rationalisation of facilities at the terminus, although there are two oil terminals slightly to the south of the area illustrated here which generate rail traffic. **(A77056/687486)**

PADSTOW

Renowned today as the location for seafood expert Rick Stein's various eating establishments, Padstow has long been both a popular destination for holidaymakers to the North Cornwall coast as well as an important fishing harbour. The North Cornwall Railway's extension to Padstow was to open on 27 March 1899. The line was controlled and operated by the London & South Western Railway. When opened the station was provided with a station building (which included a house for the stationmaster), signalbox, long fish shed (reflecting the importance of fishing to the community and to the prosperity of the line) and goods shed. The turntable was

added shortly afterwards. The location was further modified before the outbreak of World War 1 by the addition of the carriage siding, located between the station and fish shed, and the completion of the South Jetty, with its two long sidings.

The large fish shed was rebuilt by the Southern Railway in the early 1930s and it is about this time that the first of these two photographs records the scene. This was the period when, arguably, railway traffic to Padstow was at its peak. The dramatic decline in the railway's fortunes is all too apparent in the 'Now' photograph; although the South Jetty and harbour remain, the railway that once served the town is no more.

Although there was modifications to the site after the 'Then' photograph was taken — most notably the enlargement of the turntable to handle Bulleid Pacifics — traffic by the early 1950s was in decline. By 1959, the siding serving the fish shed was taken out of use whilst in January 1963 the line was transferred from Southern to Western Region control. The decline of the line became

gradually terminal; freight was withdrawn on 7 September 1964 followed by most through services to Waterloo. On 9 January 1966 the signalbox became redundant and the last through services to London were withdrawn in September 1966. On 1 October 1966 the line between Halwill Junction and Wadebridge — the old LSWR route via Launceston — closed, resulting in access to Padstow being solely via Bodmin in the period up to final closure on 30 January 1967.

As can be seen, there are today few traces that the railway ever served this Cornish port. However, close examination reveals that the former station building with stationmaster's house is still extant. There are proposals by the preserved Bodmin & Wenford Railway to extend beyond Boscarne Junction towards Wadebridge and Padstow; whether these plans will ever come to fruition, however, must be doubtful given the fact that much of the trackbed of the closed line is now a popular cycle route.

(C18141[39766]/684339)

PENISTONE

Then: 26 March 1964
Now: 13 January 2001

Viewed looking eastwards, this pair of photographs shows the approaches to Penistone, to the south of Huddersfield, from above the Woodhead route towards Manchester (1). Penistone station (2) sits at Huddersfield Junction between the Woodhead route and the line from Huddersfield (3) to Sheffield (4), coming over Penistone Viaduct (7). In the distance the line towards Barnsley (5) from Barnsley Junction can be seen crossing a short viaduct. On the Woodhead route, the small goods shed (6) can be seen.

The first railway to serve Penistone was the Sheffield, Ashton-under-Lyne & Manchester (forerunner of the Manchester, Sheffield & Lincolnshire and later the Great Central), which opened between Dunford Bridge and Sheffield on 14 July 1845. The route bisected the Pennines through the famous Woodhead Tunnel, one of the marvels of the early railway age, which opened later in

1845, thus paving the way for the first railway link between Manchester and Sheffield. The Huddersfield & Sheffield Junction Railway (later Lancashire & Yorkshire Railway) was authorised to build a line from Huddersfield to Penistone in 1845; the line was opened on 1 July 1850. The MS&LR line to Barnsley from Barnsley Junction opened to Dodworth for freight services on 15 May 1854 and to passenger services on the following 1 July. The station at Penistone illustrated here was the result of a relocation in 1874, which saw the facility move 200yd to the west and to the junction. The viaduct, prominent on the line towards Huddersfield, was the victim of a disaster in 1916 when part of it collapsed; this required the construction of a temporary station to the north of it whilst the damage was repaired. The line through Penistone and thence towards Barnsley and Sheffield was electrified as part of the Woodhead scheme, with services being introduced in the early 1950s — freight from Penistone to Wath running for the first time in 1952 although the full service was not inaugurated until the completion of the new Woodhead Tunnel in 1954.

Passenger services were withdrawn from the Hadfield-Penistone line on 5 January 1970, although the line remained open for freight traffic and occasionally for diverted passenger trains until complete closure on 20 July 1981. The line to Barnsley also lost its passenger services on 5 January 1970, but these were to be reinstated on 16 May 1983 when services were diverted away from the existing line south of Penistone (via Deepcar) to Sheffield. At this time the line south from Penistone to Deepcar was to close completely. Today, Penistone is served by passenger services run by Northern Spirit of the Huddersfield-Barnsley-Sheffield route. The line has been singled, although Penistone has a loop and retains two platforms. Ironically, 20 years after the complete closure

of the Woodhead route, active consideration is being given to its possible reopening with a number of the applicants for the new trans-Pennine franchise including reopening of the route as part of their bid. The contemporary view shows that the trackbed is largely intact, although housing has been constructed on part of the coal yard illustrated in the 'Then' photograph. A notable survival is the old goods shed, which can be seen surrounded by more recent commercial property in the centre. Another survival, visible at the junction, is the old MS&LR signalbox; this originally dated from 1888, although its lever frame was installed in the early 1950s.
(A124523/687489)

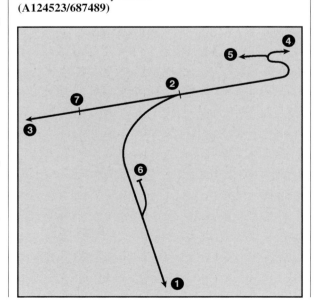

PONTYPRIDD

Then: 16 August 1955
Now: 1 May 2000

Taken looking eastwards, this pair of photographs shows the junction at the north end of Pontypridd station. The line heading northwestwards runs to Treherbert, whilst that heading north serves Aberdare. All the lines illustrated here were controlled by the Taff Vale Railway prior to the Grouping, when they passed to the Great Western. Pontypridd was also served by the Barry Railway and the Alexandra (Newport & South Wales) Docks & Railway, but neither of these companies' facilities is illustrated here.

The Taff Vale Railway was incorporated on 21 June 1836 and the official launch of work on the line occurred at Pontypridd on 16 August 1837 when the first stone was laid on the bridge across the Rhondda on the line towards Aberdare. The line through Pontypridd — known as Newbridge Junction until March 1866 — was opened as a single track between Cardiff and Navigation House (later known as Abercynon) on 9 October 1840. The line through Pontypridd was doubled in 1847. Authorisation for the line towards Treherbert and Maerdy through the Rhondda Valley was obtained in 1846, but work progressed slowly and the lines were opened in stages from the late 1840s onwards. The station illustrated here was the result of a major reconstruction in 1907, which saw the facilities considerably expanded. Under Great Western ownership, the station was renamed Pontypridd Central in 1924 to distinguish it from the ex-Barry Railway station which became Pontypridd Graig on 1 July

that year. When the latter closed on 10 July 1930, the ex-Taff vale station reverted to plain Pontypridd.

Today, Pontypridd remains the junction for the passenger services, operated by the Cardiff Railway Co, between Cardiff and Treherbert, Aberdare and Merthyr Tydfil. As can be seen, Pontypridd North Junction has been considerably reduced and the facilities provided by the station have also been curtailed, with now only two (bi-directional) platforms in operation. The freight yard

visible in the foreground of the 1955 photograph is another casualty, its site now being occupied by the inevitable car park. The station underwent modernisation in the early 1970s. Although most of the South Wales coalfield was to close by the late 1980s, the one deep-level pit to survive in the region, Tower at Hirwaun, is served by coal trains over the route through Pontypridd to Aberdare.
(R25338/685318)

PORTHCAWL

if this does occur then services will be diverted to serve Rochdale town centre. The Bacup line, however, and the extensive freight facilities have not been as fortunate. Passenger services over the Bacup line ceased on 16 June 1947 and the line closed completely north of Facit on 11 October 1954. The section from Whitworth north to Facit closed completely on 12 August 1963 whilst the final section from Rochdale East Junction to Whitworth closed completely on 21 August 1967. As a town heavily dependent upon the cotton industry, the collapse in Britain's traditional industries has hit Rochdale hard, with many of the town's mills disappearing. The lack of freight is all to evident, whilst the station has also been much reduced over the years.
(16784/685208)

RUGBY

Then: 7 August 1961
Now: 19 April 2000

Viewed looking northwards, with the impressive station (1) in the foreground, the scale of the railway infrastructure at the north end of Rugby is all too apparent in these views. From the south (2), the lines pass through the station passing the factory of GEC on the east side and the goods shed on the west. From Rugby, lines headed northwards to Leicester (3; representing the Midland's presence in the town), to Stafford (5) at Trent Valley Junction (4), to Birmingham (6) and to Leamington Spa (7) at Leamington Branch Junction (8). To the south of the station — and thus out of view — were the lines towards Market Harborough (opened 1 May 1850), to

Northampton (opened to passenger services on
1 December 1881) and to London (opened 9 April 1838).
These all served the station illustrated here; there was a
second station, again to the south of this view — Rugby
Central — which opened on 15 March 1899.

Of the lines illustrated here, the first to open was the
London & Birmingham which opened on 9 April 1838.
This was followed on 30 June 1840 by the opening of the
line to Leicester and on 1 September 1847 by the line to
Stafford. The branch to Leamington Spa opened on
1 March 1851.

The contemporary shot shows that, despite some
contraction, Rugby remains an important railway junction.
However, work was on progress at the time to remove
much of the station's overall roof and, to the east of the
line, the old GEC works has also sadly diminished in
scale since the early 1960s. This contraction has, to a
certain extent, been countered by the dramatic growth in
the cement business, which is out of the picture to the
northwest. Of the lines that have closed, that to
Leamington Spa lost its passenger services on 15 June
1959 and closed beyond Marton Junction on 4 April 1966.
The rump of the line was retained until August 1985 to
serve a cement works at Southam; a short spur is still
extant at Rugby, however, to serve New Bilton cement
works. On 1 January 1962 the old MR line to Leicester
saw its passenger services withdrawn and was closed
completely. Today a short spur is retained, as can be seen
in the photograph and the trackbed can be clearly seen
heading northwards over the viaduct. The major change to

the infrastructure has come with the electrification of the
West Coast main line. Electrification of the Trent Valley
line south from Crewe reached Rugby on 16 November
1964. The section south from Rugby to Euston
commenced operation on 6 November 1965. The Rugby-
Birmingham-Wolverhampton route was completed on
6 December 1966.
(A94405/685214)

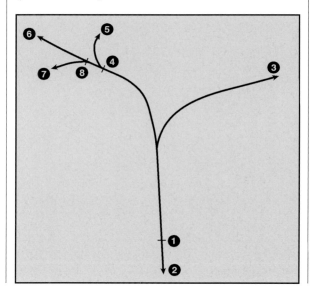

RYDE (ISLE OF WIGHT)

194

Then: 29 June 1961
Now: 1 May 2000

Stretching half a mile into the Solent, Ryde Pier is one of the most impressive piers in the country. For railway enthusiasts it is all the more impressive in that it represents the northernmost terminus of the railways that serve the Isle of Wight. The pier was opened in 1814 and was provided with a horse tramway along its length (opened on 29 August 1864), thence through the town, linking in with the Isle of Wight Railway's route southwards from Ryde St Johns Road, a line which had opened on 23 August 1864. On 5 April 1880, the Isle of Wight Railway opened its extension from St Johns Road to Esplanade and this was further extended along the length of the pier on 12 July 1880. The pier provided a deep water berth for the ferries from Portsmouth and the island's popularity grew immeasurably during the late 19th century as its reputation was enhanced by Queen

Victoria's residence at Osborne House. At the Grouping in 1923, the lines on the Isle of Wight passed to the Southern Railway and thus to BR (Southern Region) in 1948.

Taken looking southwards, the full extent of the pier is visible in these two photographs. In the earlier view, taken when the island's railway network was substantially more intact than today, it is possible to see two trains in the Pier Head station, along with four vessels, including one paddle-steamer. The 1960s were to prove a decade of both decline and investment for the island's network; much of the system was to close, the exception being the line between Pier Head and Shanklin, which route was to be

electrified using old London Transport tube stock (to cope with the slightly undersize loading gauge). Electric services were inaugurated in early 1967.

Today, more modern, but still second-hand ex-LT tube stock, has replaced the original 1967 stock. The line, however, continues to function and represents the smallest franchise offered under railway privatisation. Currently, Island Line, a subsidiary of Stagecoach, holds the franchise. As can be seen in the contemporary view, the most dramatic changes see the increased use of the pier head for parking and the loss of the pier head buildings. **(A91812/685721)**

SALISBURY

Then: 11 May 1965
Now: 1 May 2000

A space of almost exactly 35 years separates these two views of Salisbury in Wiltshire. Viewed looking east, the ex-GWR and ex-LSWR lines from Wilton Junction head towards the station. On the southside of the ex-LSWR lines (on the extreme right of the 'Then' photograph) can be seen part of the steam shed that served the city. This structure was opened by the LSWR in 1901 and replaced an earlier shed that was closed when the station was rebuilt between 1900 and 1902. The shed as illustrated here had been reroofed by BR in 1954. Adjacent to the ex-LSWR station — the result of the rebuilding work of the early 20th century — can be seen the site of the

ex-GWR passenger station in the city; this had closed to passenger services on 12 September 1932, when services were diverted to the SR station, but remained as a goods yard. Beyond the station, the main line continues east towards Fisherton Tunnel and the junction for the line southwards to Southampton. Between the station and Fisherton Tunnel there was a short branch — built under the auspices of the Salisbury Railway & Market House Co — linking the railway to the city's market house. This freight-only line opened in 1856 — with a revised junction in 1859 — and remained independently owned throughout its life, although operated by the LSWR and its successors. The line survived in part until the late 1960s to serve a warehouse, having been cut back from its original terminus on 1 June 1964.

The first railway to serve Salisbury was the branch from the south, which opened to a station at Milford on 1 March 1847; this station closed on 2 May 1859 with services extended via a link to a new station constructed in connection with the LSWR's new line westwards. The LSWR opened its route from Andover to Salisbury on 1 May 1857 and westwards towards Yeovil on 2 May 1859 (contemporaneously with the new station). Broad

gauge interest in Salisbury came with the opening of the Wilts, Somerset & Weymouth Railway — later GWR — on 30 June 1856.

Today, the steam shed is no more, being closed on 9 July 1967. After standing derelict for some years, the building was subsequently demolished, although the site is still undeveloped. In contrast, however, a new depot has been constructed on the site of the former GWR goods shed to service the Class 159 DMUs introduced on to the Waterloo-Salisbury-Exeter service. This opened in 1993 and is currently in the hands of South West Trains, although this may change with the refranchising proposals covering the area and the possible creation of a Wessex franchise. The ex-GWR route from Wilton Junction has been closed with traffic transferred to the ex-LSWR line; track, however, remains at the eastern end to serve the new depot and at the Wilton Junction end to serve an English China Clays' terminal at Quidhampton. Salisbury station itself remains largely unchanged and continues to act as an important junction for services from Southampton and from Westbury.
(A145915/685227)

SCARBOROUGH

Then: 10 August 1972
Now: 25 January 2001

Although Scarborough had long been a place of strategic importance, with its castle, it was the coming of the railway that provided one of the great stimuli to the growth of the town in the 19th century, as the residents of the textile towns of Yorkshire discovered the bracing effect of the North Sea coast. Looking first at the 'Then' photograph, Scarborough Central (1) dominates the centre of the scene, with the line stretching southwest towards Seamer Junction and York (2). As it heads out of the station, the line passes the junction for the line to Whitby (5) and the site of the already closed Excursion (Londesborough Road) station (3). From Scarborough, the

of Sheffield) through to Tapton Junction at Chesterfield. The new Midland station was opened at the same time, although the station illustrated in both of these photographs dates back to rebuilding work undertaken to the design of Charles Trubshaw in 1904. Adjacent to the station — which acquired the suffix 'City' in 1950 and was then known as 'Sheffield Midland from 1951 until 1970 — is the Pond Street goods depot. Also of transport interest in the photograph is the triangular shed building situated to the southwest of the station; this is the Shoreham Street depot of Sheffield Corporation Transport. In 1959, Sheffield became the last major English city still to operate tramcars and one of the fleet's Roberts-built tramcars, dating from the early 1950s can be seen running on the road parallel to the railway line to the west of the station.

Sheffield's last conventional tramcars operated on 8 October 1960. However, this was not to be the end of light rail in the city; a second generation network was opened on 21 March 1994 and evidence of the new system — now operated under franchise by Stagecoach — can be seen running parallel to the railway on the east side of the station. Sheffield station itself is remarkably unchanged in 40 years, retaining much of the structure that existed in 1959. Pond Street goods yard is, however, no more, having closed on 19 September 1960. Today, Sheffield remains an important railway centre, with services provided by a number of Train Operating Companies.
(A77734/685232)

SHEPTON MALLET

Then: 10 June 1964
Now: 1 May 2000

The Somerset town of Shepton Mallet was served by two railways: the Somerset & Dorset heading north from Evercreech Junction towards Bath and the Great Western (East Somerset Railway) line from Witham towards Yatton through the Cheddar Valley. The S&D station was provided the suffix 'Charlton Road' in September 1949, after Nationalisation, whilst the ex-GWR one became 'High Street'. The East Somerset Railway opened as a broad gauge line from Witham to Shepton Mallet on 9 November 1858 and thence to Wells on 1 March 1862. The ESR (along with the associated Cheddar Valley Railway) became part of the GWR. The East Somerset

Railway was converted to standard gauge in 1874. The Somerset & Dorset line northwards through Shepton Mallet opened on 20 July 1874.

The 'Then' photograph records the scene as it appeared in mid-1964. By this date passenger services over the ex-GWR line between Yatton and Witham had already ceased — on 7 September 1963 — although freight was still operational throughout. The Somerset & Dorset line was also still open, although its time was running out. Both the ex-GWR line (passing over the second route) and the S&D are clearly visible in this view, as are the facilities — goods shed, signalbox and water tower — at the ex-S&D station. Although freight facilities had been withdrawn from Charlton Road on 10 June 1963, there remain wagons to the south of the goods yard.

Shepton Mallet is anther depressing location for those interested in railways, with virtually no trace evident of either railway route today. The major reference point is the housing estate which appeared new in 1964 and which has been considerably extended over the past 35 years. The population of the town is now much greater than it was in the early 1960s but the primary form of transport for the majority is now the all-conquering car. The Somerset & Dorset line closed completely on 7 March 1966 whilst freight services between Cranmore and Cheddar — the line closed north of Cheddar in late 1964 — ceased on 1 April 1969. There is little remaining of the erstwhile S&D route, although it is still possible to identify the trackbed of the ex-GWR route. Further to the east, part of the East Somerset Railway now forms the modern and preserved East Somerset Railway (at Cranmore) and the easternmost section (to Witham) provides a link to the Foster Yeoman quarry at Merehead. **(A131372/685247)**

SHOTTON

Then: 1961
Now: 25 January 2001

Situated on the south side of the River Dee as it approaches its estuary, Shotton possessed two stations, which, as can be seen in these photographs, were closely related. In the centre can be seen Shotton (High Level) (1), which is situated on the line between Wrexham (3) and Hawarden (6). The second station, Shotton (Low Level) (2) is on the main line between Chester (7) and Holyhead (4). Just to the north of the railway bridge, a junction can be seen with a track (5) heading westwards;

this provided a link towards Connah's Quay.

The first line through Shotton was the Chester & Holyhead Railway (later the London & North Western), which opened from Chester to Bangor for passenger services on 1 May 1848 and to freight on the following 1 June. Initially there was no station provided at Shotton; this was not to be opened until 1907. The second line to serve Shotton was the Wrexham, Mold & Connah's Quay Railway. This line was authorised on 18 August 1882 but was not finally to open until 31 March 1890 at the same time as the one-mile freight-only branch to serve Connah's Quay. When opened, the WM&CQR's station was known as 'Connah's Quay &

Shotton' and opened in 1891; the two stations did not become 'High Level' and 'Low Level' until the early 1950s. The WM&CQR, never a strong operator financially, was eventually to fall into the hands of the Great Central Railway (in 1901) and thus, at Grouping in 1923, it became part of the LNER.

Shotton (Low Level) was closed on 14 February 1966 but was reopened on 21 August 1972 after it had been reconstructed to accommodate the reduction from four to two of the running lines. Today passenger services on the Wrexham-Bidston line are in the hands of First North Western, whilst the Chester-Holyhead line sees trains operated by Virgin, First North Western and Wales & West. The freight-only link to Connah's Quay has disappeared, although there remains other freight activity in the area. As can be seen, the reopened station was built on the site of the original, although the facilities offered are much more basic than those available 40 years ago. The only major change here is the loss of the freight-only spur towards Connah's Quay, although the trackbed of the link is readily identifiable.
(A93718/687008)

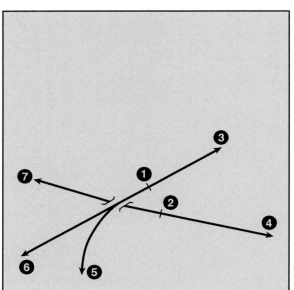

Then: 14 April 1972
Now: 20 May 2000

Regarded as the gateway to the Dales, Skipton's importance was reflected in the construction of the castle, which guarded the route through the Pennines from the Aire Valley in the east towards the north Lancashire coast. That the Aire Valley represented an essential trans-Pennine route was illustrated in the 18th century by the construction of the Leeds-Liverpool Canal through the valley, visible in the foreground of both photographs. It was also inevitable that railway promoters would see the Aire Valley route as a relatively easy alignment for providing a link between the industrial West Riding and Lancashire. The first railway to reach Skipton was the Leeds & Bradford Railway (later Midland Railway) which opened from Keighley to Skipton on 8 September 1847 and thence to Colne on 2 October 1848. The line towards Hellifield was opened on 30 July 1849 whilst Skipton's importance as a railway junction was further enhanced by the construction of the line towards Embsay and Ilkley, which opened on 1 October 1888. This route not only allowed local services between the two towns but also provided a useful diversionary routes for long-distance services between Leeds and the northwest and Scotland.

The first of these two photographs shows the facilities at Skipton in the early 1970s. The station was relocated to its current position in April 1876. The single-track line towards Rylstone (on the Grassington branch; opened from Embsay Junction to Grassington on 29 July 1902 and closed to passenger services on 22 September 1930) can be seen heading over the main line northwards. This was the remaining section of the erstwhile route to Ilkley, which had lost its passenger services on 22 March 1965 and which had been closed completely east of Embsay Junction on 5 July 1965. To the north of the station, the town retains significant freight facilities. To the west of the station — out of view — the line towards Colne closed on 2 February 1970.

Three decades on, Skipton is still an important railway destination. Electrification of the line through the Aire Valley to Leeds brings Northern Spirit's EMUs to the town, whilst services towards Lancashire and Carlisle are in the hands of the same TOC's DMUs. Although the Rylstone branch remains — and there are hopes that the preserved Embsay & Bolton Abbey Railway may one day expand its services into the town over the route — other freight facilities have disappeared and the site of the goods yard has been redeveloped.
(A225494/685731)

SLEAFORD

Then: 20 March 1951
Now: 24 January 2001

Sleaford is one of three Lincolnshire junctions to feature in this collection and like both Gainsborough and Spalding is now much reduced in scale. Taken looking southeastwards, this pair of photographs show the approaches to Sleaford from the east and the lines heading through to the station (1) towards Grantham (2) and Lincoln (3) which diverge at Sleaford West Junction (4). The line towards Lincoln will head towards the north and Sleaford North Junction, where it will meet the Sleaford avoiding line. Heading east from the station, three sets of lines can be distinguished. The northernmost of these are heading towards Boston (5), the middle set towards

Spalding (6) and the southernmost towards Bourne (7). The line towards Spalding will connect with the Sleaford avoiding line at Sleaford South Junction.

The first railway to serve the town was Boston, Sleaford & Midland Counties (later Great Northern) Railway that opened its route from Grantham on 16 June 1857. The line was extended onwards to Boston on 13 April 1859. The GNR line to Bourne was opened on 2 January 1872. The route southwards to Spalding opened on 6 March 1882 and that to Lincoln on the following 1 August; these sections of track, along with the Sleaford avoiding line, were controlled by the Great Northern & Great Eastern Joint. By the date of the 'Then' photograph, the Bourne line had already lost its passenger services, these being withdrawn on 22 September 1930 although the line was still operational for freight traffic.

The remains of the line towards Bourne closed completely between when final traffic was withdrawn from the Sleaford East Junction-Billingborough & Horbling section on 28 July 1956. Elsewhere, however, Sleaford has retained its other railway links, although the avoiding line is no longer regularly used. Passenger services, provided by Central Trains, operate between Grantham and Skegness and between Spalding and Lincoln. Inevitably, there has been considerable rationalisation of track, although the station retains its three platforms. As can be seen, Sleaford station is largely unchanged over 50 years, with its platforms and buildings intact. Also still extant in this view are the goods shed at

the western end of the station and two signalboxes (East — built by GNR in 1882 and closest to the camera — and West — built by the GNR in 1880). To the east of the station, past Southgate Crossing, the route has been reduced to single track.
(A35001/687612)

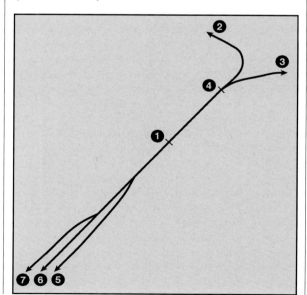

SNOWDON

Then: 13 June 1950
Now: 13 January 2001

Snowdon is, at 3,559ft, the highest mountain in England and Wales and from the late 1860s, with the opening of Carnarvon & Llanberis Railway, its popularity as a tourist attraction grew rapidly. This pair of views shows the terminus of the Snowdon Mountain Railway and, in the earlier of the two views, one of the line's steam locomotives. Although there were proposals from the 1870s for the construction of a railway from Llanberis to the summit, these fell foul of the then owner of the mountain, George William Duff Assheton-Smith. However, by the 1890s, his attitude changed and, with the registering of the Snowdon Mountain Tramroad & Hotels Co Ltd in 1894, work commenced on the construction of the line in December of that year. Three locomotives were supplied in 1895 by the Swiss company of Schweizerische Lokomotiv und Maschinenfabrik of Winterthür along with four coaches from the Lancaster Railway Carriage & Wagon Co. Before the line opened at Easter 1896, two further locomotives and two coaches had also been acquired.

Built to a gauge of 800mm (2ft 7.5in) and some 4.75 miles in length, the line has ruling gradient of 1 in 5.5 and power is transmitted from the locomotive via rack and pinion. Although the line had undergone rigorous testing prior to opening, the first day of public operation resulted in a fatal accident and the suspension of services for 12 months whilst the rack was modified. The line reopened on 19 April 1897. The station building at the summit illustrated here was designed by the architect Clough Williams-Ellis — better known perhaps as the architect behind Portmeirion — and opened in 1936. By this date the railway's fleet of locomotives had been further strengthened and company's name had been changed (in 1928) to Snowdon Mountain Railway Ltd.

Today, the Snowdon Mountain Railway remains a highly popular means of reaching the summit of the mountain, although services are only operated between March and the end of October and can be suspended in adverse weather. Britain's only — at the moment — rack railway is still primarily steam operated, although the company does possess four diesel locomotives. In the now shot — taken when the Mountain peak was well covered with snow — the 1936-built station stands alone in the winter landscape.
(R13135C/687507)

SOUTHPORT

Then: 26 July 1938
Now: 10 January 2001

The railway age helped to create a large number of coastal holiday resorts; of these the Lancashire town of Southport was one that experienced rapid growth as a consequence of its proximity to Liverpool and its attractiveness to visitors from the West Riding. By the date of the first of these two photographs, the town was served by two terminal stations: Lord Street, in the foreground, controlled by the Cheshire Lines Committee, and Chapel Street, controlled by the LMS (ex-Lancashire & Yorkshire), which can be seen in the background.

The first railway to serve Southport was the Liverpool, Crosby & Southport Railway — later part of the L&YR

— which opened to the terminus at Chapel Street in August 1851. This was followed by the Manchester & Southport Railway, which opened its line from Wigan to Chapel Street on 9 April 1855. The East Lancashire Railway, another future constituent of the L&YR, ran into Southport along the same lines as the M&SR from Burscough Bridge, although it constructed its own station, London Street, adjacent to Chapel Street, which was eventually absorbed into an enlarged Chapel Street when the latter was rebuilt after the various companies merged. Chapel Street was also served by trains coming off the West Lancashire Railway route from Preston; this line, opened to Southport Central on 4 September 1882, saw its services diverted into Chapel Street on 1 April 1901. Opened under the name of the Southport & Cheshire Lines Extension, the long CLC branch from Aintree

opened to Lord Street on 1 September 1884. Chapel Street station was extended in 1901, whilst the L&YR line between Liverpool and Southport via Crosby was electrified in 1904.

As is clearly evident in the 'Then' photograph, the provision at both of the town's passenger termini was impressive. However, by World War 2, the fortunes of the town as holiday resort were numbered for rail-borne passengers, despite the inauguration of the town's flower show in 1924. The contemporary shot shows clearly how much of the town's railway infrastructure has disappeared. The most notable casualty is the complete closure of Lord Street station. Passenger services ceased over the CLC route to the station on 7 January 1952, and the section between Lord Street and Altcar & Hillhouse was to close completely on 7 July of the same year. Initially Lord Street station was used as a bus station, although the site has now been redeveloped; note, however, that the station frontage and clock tower still remain. Another casualty was the West Lancashire Railway line towards Preston, passenger services over the route ceased on 7 September 1964, at which time the line closed completely. Chapel Street remains with DMU services eastbound towards Wigan, operated by First North Western, and southbound towards Liverpool, operated by Merseyrail electrics. Limited siding accommodation is provided in the 'V' at the station throat, whilst to the north of the line towards Wigan is the Excursion platform. Located adjacent to this site was the Steamport Transport Museum, which occupied Southport Derby Road shed (which is just visible at the extreme top of the 'Then' photograph. The shed, which was reroofed in 1953, closed in 1966 and was then occupied by preservationists. Preservation was to last until 1997 when, due to the condition of the roof, the decision was taken to close and relocate.
(58486/687620)

SPALDING

Then: 16 April 1947
Now: 19 June 2000

As can be seen from the first of these two photographs, Spalding — a town famous for its spring flower festival — was also once a railway junction of some importance. Bisecting the photograph, running from north to south is the ex-Great Northern line to Boston (2) and Peterborough (8). At the centre is Spalding station (1). At Spalding North Junction (4) the ex-Great Northern & Great Eastern line heads towards Sleaford (3). South of the station, the ex-Midland & Great Northern line heads from Bourne (10) towards King's Lynn (6). Passing under the M&GN route is the GN&GEJt line towards March (7) whilst connections from Spalding station — Holbeach Lane Junction (11) — to the M&GN are made at Welland Bank Junction (5) and Cuckoo Junction (12). Also visible — and reflecting the MR's involvement in the M&GN — is the ex-Midland goods yard (9).

The first line to open through Spalding was the GNR route from Peterborough to Boston. This opened on 17 October 1848. The GNR-controlled Norwich & Spalding Railway opened between Spalding and Holbeach on 15 November 1858 and thence to Sutton Bridge on 3 July 1862; another element of the future M&GN opened

northwards to Long Melford. There the line divided, one branch heading north, serving Lavenham and Bury St Edmunds, and the other west towards Haverhill and Cambridge.

By the time of the 'Then' photograph, the area had already started to lose some of its railways and diesel traction had arrived with DMUs being introduced over the route on 1 January 1959. Note the Brush Type 2 (later Class 31) in the goods yard. Passenger services over the line from Long Melford to Bury St Edmunds ceased on 10 April 1961. By 1964 freight services were also under threat; those south of Sudbury were withdrawn on 2 November 1964, whilst those north of Sudbury succumbed on 31 October 1966, at which time the line into Sudbury Old was also closed. Passenger services north of Sudbury to Shelford Junction, Cambridge, ceased on 6 March 1967, leaving Sudbury — by now an

unstaffed station — as the northern terminus of the branch from Marks Tey.

There were real threats during the early 1970s that this remaining branch would also be closed and a preservation society was established at Chappel & Wakes Colne station, to the south, to take over the line if final closure did occur. In the event, as can be seen from the more recent photograph, the line did survive, although the station facilities at Sudbury are now much more rudimentary than they were in 1964. The 1865 station has now been demolished and the site used for a car park for the adjacent leisure centre. North of Sudbury the trackbed has been taken over for use as a cycle route, whilst today services are provided by the modern Great Eastern, whose DMUs link Sudbury to Colchester.
(A124738/684536)

SWANSEA

Then: 8 September 1971
Now: 1 May 2000

Whilst Swansea possessed a complex railway network with services provided by three of the pre-Grouping companies — the Midland, the Great Western and the London & North Western railways — by the time the first of these photographs was taken, the city's facilities had been much reduced. These views, taken looking westwards, show the ex-GWR Swansea (High Street) station. By the date of the 'Then' photograph, all the city's passenger services had been concentrated into this station, with the closure of the ex-LNWR Victoria and ex-MR St Thomas stations in 1964 and 1950 respectively. Visible in the station is a rake of coaches

with a Class 08 shunter at the country end and a five-car DMU. On the east side of the station can be seen the trackbed of the line that ran from High Street parallel to the North Dock and Wind Street Junction to form a connection with the LNWR at South Dock; this line was closed completely on 1 November 1965. The South Wales Railway opened from Neath to Swansea in 1850 and the station as illustrated here was the result of remodelling in 1934.

Today, Swansea station remains very much as it did 30 years ago; although the concourse area was modernised in 1972/73 to provide a travel centre, this facility is not evident from the air. What is clear, however, is that part of the platform canopy on the easternmost platform has been curtailed whilst the goods yard and signalbox evident in the 1971 photograph have been eliminated. Swansea station now possesses four platforms with carriage sidings located slightly to the north. Passenger services are currently in the hands of First Great Western and Virgin Cross-Country — both handling long-distance services — whilst local trains are the province of the Wales & West franchise. As with other locations in Wales, the franchise arrangements are liable to change with the creation of a single franchise covering all local services within the Principality.
(**A215804/685250**)

THORNABY

Then: 14 March 1962
Now: 25 January 2001

Located to the east of Thornaby station, on the line from Darlington to Middlesbrough, and to the south of the large Tees Yard and River Tees, Thornaby shed was one of a number of sheds constructed in the late 1950s and represented BR's final essay in the construction of a steam shed, although by the date of its construction the 1955 Modernisation Plan was already coming to fruition and it was clear that steam only had a relatively short life on the main line. As built, the shed consisted of two structures: the polygonal roundhouse with turntable on the west and the 13-road — of which nine were through — shed to the east. Coded 51L by the North Eastern Region, the new

shed opened on 5 June 1958 and replaced earlier sheds at Middlesbrough and Newport. Its area of operation was further expanded in 1959 when it took over duties previously undertaken at Stockton and Haverton Hill. At the time the first of these two photographs was taken steam locomotives were still present in significant numbers, although their days at Thornaby were numbered.

Thornaby shed lost its steam allocation in December 1964, at which time the roundhouse ceased to be used for locomotive work and started a second life as a wagon repair shop. With the recoding of all BR sheds in the 1970s, Thornaby became TE. As can be seen in the contemporary photograph, Thornaby is still active as a depot, although the roundhouse was demolished shortly after its second life ceased in 1988. It is, however, still possible to see clearly the foundations of the structure and locate the turntable pit. Elsewhere, notable changes include the fact that the main Middlesbrough-Stockton road is now a dual-carriageway and the Mandale Marshes Race Course, visible in the foreground of the 'Then' shot, has disappeared.
(A98447/687581)

TOTTENHAM

Then: 1923
Now: 20 May 2000

Viewed looking east and with the Lea Navigation running north-south, this pair of photographs records the changing scene at Tottenham in northeast London. In the foreground, running from west to east, is the Tottenham &

Forest Gate Joint line from South Tottenham to Woodgrange Park; this line was originally owned by the London, Tilbury & Southend and Midland railways and thus passed to the exclusive control of the Midland when the MR took over the LT&SR on 1 January 1912. Heading from north to south is the Great Eastern Railway's Lea Valley line from Stratford through Lea Bridge towards Ponders End. Tottenham (Hale) station can be seen

towards the left of the photograph. This photograph was taken in 1923, shortly after the Grouping, when the MR line passed to the LMS and the GER route to the LNER. The extreme east of the view shows Lockwood Reservoir, whilst the middle of the 'Then' photograph shows a large camouflaged factory.

Tottenham (Hale) was one of the original stations opened by the Northern & Eastern Railway Co. This railway was incorporated on 4 July 1836 to construct a line from Cambridge to Islington. Financial exigencies forced the company to divert its approaches to London so that a junction could be made with the Eastern Counties at Stratford. The line from Stratford to Broxbourne, including the station at Tottenham, which opened on 15 September 1840, was originally built to a gauge of 5ft, but this was converted to standard gauge in the autumn of 1844, by which time the N&E had been leased to the ECR. Both were ultimately to form part of the Great Eastern. The Tottenham & Forest Gate Railway — some

six miles in length — was authorised in 1890, being jointly promoted by the LT&SR and the MR to provide a link between the lines of the two companies. It was opened throughout on 9 July 1894.

The old GER station was replaced in the late 1960s when the new Victoria Line of London Underground was opened with an interchange at Tottenham Hale. Note that most of the industrial activity visible in 1923 has disappeared although odd patches, particularly to the west, are still identifiable. Today, the line between Woodgrange Park and South Tottenham is used by the DMUs of Silverlink as part of the Gospel Oak-Barking service, whilst the erstwhile GER route, which was electrified on 5 May 1969, sees EMU services operated by West Anglia Great Northern to Stansted Airport — with Tottenham Hale being the only intermediate stop between the airport and Liverpool Street — and to Hertford East and Cambridge.
(6778/685733)

TOWCESTER

Then: 18 September 1964
Now: 15 March 2000

The history of Britain's railways is littered with the construction of small country junctions; one of these was Towcester, in Northamptonshire, where the Stratford on Avon & Midland Junction Railway's line from Broom to Ravenstone Wood Junction (on the Midland Railway line from Northampton to Bedford) crossed the SMJR's second line from Blisworth to Cockley Brake Junction (near Banbury).

The railway — under the aegis of the Northampton & Banbury Junction Railway — first reached Towcester in May 1866 with the opening of the line from Blisworth; this was extended to Cockley Brake Junction on 1 June

1872 (whence running powers were exercised to take services into Banbury). The line from Towcester to Stratford on Avon opened, courtesy of the East & West Junction Railway, on 1 July 1873, although this company was to struggle financially with passenger services being suspended for eight years after receivers were appointed in 1877. The next phase of railway development at Towcester came on 13 April 1891 with the opening of the line to Ravenstone Wood Junction (and in the west by the extension from Stratford to Broom) which both opened on 13 April 1891. The SMJR came about as a result of amalgamations in 1908 and 1910.

By the date of the earlier of these two photographs, services at Towcester had already been reduced. Passenger services between Blisworth and Banbury had been withdrawn on 29 October 1951 and those between Blisworth and Stratford on 7 April 1952 (at which stage Towcester closed as a passenger station). The lines, however, representing a useful east-west link remained open for freight, with the exception of the line from Towcester to Cockley Brake Junction, which closed completely on 29 October 1951. At the time the 'Then' photograph was taken even the remaining freight services had ceased; the line towards Ravenstone Wood Junction closed in June 1958, but as is evident from the photograph was still intact. The line from Blisworth to Woodford closed completely on 3 February 1964, when freight facilities were also withdrawn from the station.

Today, there is little to indicate the presence of the railway in this location. The station site has been wholly redeveloped and the road bridge to the west of the station has been demolished. Perhaps emphasising how transport priorities have changed over the past century a dual carriageway now runs east to west and the remaining trackbed, to the west of the station, is overgrown. The only certain reference points in the contemporary photograph are the alignment of the river and the white building to the west of the station site.
(A139983/684327)

TWEEDMOUTH

Then: 30 April 1949
Now: 12 January 2001

Described as Berwick on Tweed in the Aerofilms catalogue, this actually shows in the foreground Tweedmouth with, across the River Tweed to the north, Berwick on Tweed. The dramatic sweep of the East Coast main line from Edinburgh (1) through Berwick on Tweed station (2) and over the Royal Border Bridge (3) and on towards Newcastle (7) is readily apparent. Tweedmouth station (5) was the junction for the line towards Coldstream (4). Also clearly visible is the double reversal required by trains accessing Tweed Dock (6). Finally, Tweedmouth shed (8).can be identified to the south of the station. The shed dated originally to 1847 and was

reroofed in 1881. The shed was to be closed by BR on 19 June 1966 and sold for private use.

The railway reached Tweedmouth from the south, courtesy of the Newcastle & Berwick Railway, on 29 March 1847. The railway at Berwick had already opened on 22 June 1846 under the auspices of the North British Railway. A temporary bridge was provided over the Tweed, opening on 10 October 1848, and the Royal Border Bridge was completed for freight traffic on 20 July 1850 and for passenger traffic on 29 August of the same year. The bridge, designed by Robert Stephenson, has 28 arches and rises 126ft above the high water mark. The branch westwards to Coldstream and Kelso opened on 27 July 1849.

Today, Tweedmouth station is no more; it closed on 15 June 1964. All that remains at Tweedmouth, apart from the now electrified ECML, are limited sidings on the up side. The line towards Coldstream also lost its passenger services on 15 June 1964. The current scene shows the electrified East Coast main line heading north-south through the site of the now-closed station at Tweedmouth. The junction for the line towards Coldstream remains, although slightly to the west — just beyond the edge of the area shown — the trackbed has been demolished. Whilst the dock is still functioning, it no longer possesses rail facilities, although it is still possible to identify the route and the short viaduct that formed part of the route to the dock is still extant. Also still standing, but no longer linked to the railway network, is the former steam shed.
(C19792/687204)

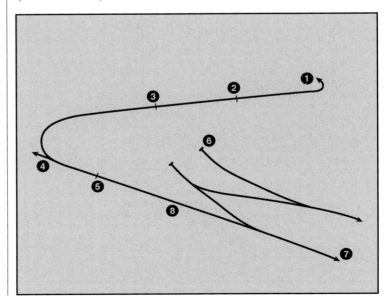

WELLINGTON (SHROPSHIRE)

Then: August 1930
Now: 30 April 2000

Viewed looking northeastwards, this view shows the important junction of Wellington in Shropshire. To the west stretches the ex-GWR/LNWR joint line towards Shrewsbury and, slightly to the west of the area illustrated here, the Great Western line towards Market Drayton headed northwards. At the extreme east of the photograph can be seen Wellington station with, slightly to the north, the GWR engine shed. East of Wellington, the GWR main line headed towards Birmingham, whilst the LNWR headed northeastwards towards Stafford. Wellington was also the terminus for the GWR line southwards to Buildwas and the LNWR branch towards Coalport. The engine shed was opened in 1876; when pictured in 1930, the shed still possessed a turntable although this was

destined to disappear during the following decade.

The lines from Shrewsbury to Oakengates (east of Wellington) and from Wellington to Stafford opened on 1 June 1849; the line from Oakengates to Wolverhampton opened on the following 12 November. The route towards Stafford was to lose its passenger services on 7 September 1964 and was progressively cut back to all traffic, the last section at the Wellington end (serving a military store at Donnington) closed in the late 1980s. The line southwards from Wellington was to open in 1857 with passenger services commencing on 2 May 1859; the line from Much Wenlock to Wellington lost its passenger services on 23 July 1962, at which time the line south from Wellington to Ketley closed completely. The ex-LNWR Coalport branch opened on 17 June 1861; it was to lose its passenger services on 2 June 1952 and to close completely between Stirchley and Coalport on 5 December 1960. The remains of the line, from Hadley Junction to Stirchley,

closed completely on 6 July 1964. The final addition to the local network came with the opening of the Wellington & Drayton Railway on 16 October 1867. This line was to lose its passenger services on 9 September 1963 and close completely on 8 May 1967.

Today, Wellington is one of the major districts of the new town of Telford although, as can be seen clearly, its railway facilities have been much reduced. The engine shed — coded 84H (1959) by British Railways — was to close on 10 August 1964 and the site has subsequently been cleared. The station, however, is remarkably unchanged in some 70 years. Following closures, the only line to survive is that from Wolverhampton to Shrewsbury, over which Central Trains provides the vast majority of services. A tenuous long-distance link remains with the Virgin West Coast service to Euston. Also now closed are the ex-LNWR (north) and ex-GWR (south) goods yards. The former has disappeared under the site of another new supermarket although much of the latter — which was the last to close — remains undeveloped. **(34033/685255)**

WESTBURY

Then: 21 June 1929
Now: 1 May 2000

It is rare in compiling a book of this nature, to find a location outside a major city where the railway infrastructure has expanded in the period since the 'Then' photograph was taken. It is even more unusual where this expansion has taken place in the freight facilities but that is the case with Westbury.

The first of these two photographs dates to the late 1920s and shows the view looking towards the northeast. The broad gauge Wilts, Somerset & Weymouth Railway (later part of the Great Western Railway from 14 March 1850) reached Westbury from Thingley Junction via Trowbridge on 5 September 1848; the line was operated by the GWR from the outset. The line was extended from Westbury to Frome on 7 October 1850 and from Westbury to Warminster on 9 September 1851. The station as illustrated here was the result of a reconstruction in 1900 as part of the building of the new main line from Patney & Chirton (on the line from Newbury to Devizes) to Westbury. The 15-mile Berks & Hants Extension Railway opened to freight services on 29 July 1900 and to passenger services on 1 October of the same year.

The first of these photographs predates the opening of the Westbury avoiding line — in 1933 — which is situated to the south of the scene recorded in the contemporary view. Today, Westbury retains the station as built in 1900 and much of the surrounding landscape is also familiar from the scene 80 years ago. Note, however, the considerably expanded siding accommodation to the west of the station. Westbury is a staging post for the block trains of stone from the Mendip quarries at Merehead and Whatley. It is also the location of an important EWS locomotive depot. Passenger services through the station are provided by First Great Western, with services from London to the West Country and, currently, Wales & West on services from Bath to Salisbury.
(C12457/685265)

WESTON SUPER MARE

Then: May 1930
Now: 1 May 2000

Although the railways did not create Weston-super-Mare as a holiday destination — the first hotel opened in 1808 some 33 years before the branch built by the Bristol & Exeter Railway opened — the development of the town was undoubtedly facilitated by the huge numbers of passengers that could reach the town by rail. The first of these photographs shows the railway facilities in 1930, just after the excursion station — Locking Road — had been extensively rebuilt and when, arguably, the influence of the railway upon the town was at its greatest. Clearly visible in the 'Then' photograph are the terminal platforms of the Locking Road excursion station alongside the curving platforms of the through Weston General station on the loop off the main line between Exeter and Bristol.

Situated between the two stations was the goods yard, which was the site of the original B&ER terminus.

Although Weston-super-Mare was initially bypassed by the B&ER main line, a 1.5 mile long branch serving the town was opened on 14 June 1841. The single-track broad-gauge line was generally horse-operated initially, but the growth of traffic meant that facilities gradually had to be increased and steam became the regular means of propulsion from 1 April 1851. The line was doubled in 1866, when the station was rebuilt, and became mixed gauge in 1875. The B&ER was to be leased to the Great Western Railway on 1 January 1876 and amalgamated with it on 1 August of the same year. The original branch and station was closed on 1 March 1884 when the new loop with through station was constructed. The 1884 station is that illustrated in the 'Then' photograph alongside the Locking Road excursion station that was rebuilt in the 1920s.

Today, Weston-super-Mare is still served by a loop off the main line between Exeter and Bristol, with passenger services provided by Virgin Cross-Country and First Great Western (long distance) and Wales & West (local). Although the main station remains largely intact — albeit the platform canopies have been rebuilt — gone are the goods yard and Locking Road excursion station. The latter closed on 6 September 1964. The town had the majority of its freight facilities withdrawn on 20 June 1966.

All evidence of the excursion platforms and goods yard have now been swept away and the area redeveloped with new roads. Although both through platforms remain in use at the station, the line on either side towards Taunton and towards Bristol has now been singled. Demonstrating that travellers still come to Weston-super-Mare in large numbers is the fact that part of the area previously occupied by the excursion station is now used as a coach park.
(P1031/685274)

WILLESDEN

Then: 9 March 1964
Now: 27 June 2000

Situated on the West Coast main line between London Euston and Watford Junction, Willesden is one of the most important junctions located on the southern part of the route. Located in the foreground are the platforms of Willesden Junction (High Level) (1), (Low Level) (2) and (Main Line) (already closed by this date; 3) stations. The West Coast main line heads towards London (10) and Watford Junction (14), whilst at West London Junction (4) the ex-LNWR line towards Kensington (9) heads southwards through Mitre Bridge Junction (15). From

Mitre Bridge Junction there is a spur towards Willesden High Level Junction (8) on the line towards Richmond (7). To the north of the view, three sets of lines head towards Kensal Green Junction (6); these are the Up and Down City lines to the north heading towards Willesden Yard (11); the Up and Down Platform lines heading into High Level station en route to Richmond and the Up and Down New lines heading into Low Level and thence to Stonebridge Park (12). Just to the east of the station, the New lines are joined by the lines from Queens Park, which are also used by the Bakerloo Line trains of London Underground. Just to the east of the Main Line platforms, at North and South Western Junction, lines diverge from the West Coast main line to serve Willesden Yards (13)

and Richmond (via Acton Wells Junction) (16). Also visible, under construction, was the depot (17) built to service the locomotives destined for use on the 25kV electrification of the West Coast route.

The first railway to serve the area was the London & Birmingham, which opened north from Euston on 20 July 1837, although it was not until 1 September 1866 that a station called Willesden Junction opened. By that date much of the local infrastructure had already been completed; the line from North & South West Junction to Kew — later rerouted to Richmond — opened to freight on 15 February 1853 and to passenger services on 1 August 1853 whilst the Hampstead Junction (owned eventually by the LNWR but operated by the North London) opened through Willesden to Camden Town on 2 February 1860. The station was rebuilt in 1894 and further extended on 15 June 1912 with the opening of platforms to serve the New Lines, which also opened on that date north of Willesden to Harrow. Bakerloo Line services reached Willesden on 10 May 1915 and were extended north to Watford Junction on 16 April 1917. The station as illustrated in the 'Then' photograph was very much the result of the 1894 rebuilding and 1912 expansion, although the LMS had reduced the number of platforms serving High Level.

Given its importance, both in its proximity to London and as a major junction, the railway presence at Willesden is still significant. The only major casualties have been the Main Line platforms — which closed on 3 December 1962 and the platforms cleared soon afterwards in connection with the electrification project — and the well-stocked freight sidings to the south of line adjacent to West London Junction. The traditional North London

line services through High Level, which now operate between Richmond and North Woolwich as part of the Silverlink franchise, have been supplemented by Anglia Railways' service from East Anglia to Basingstoke. Low Level station — note the improved bus-interchange facilities — is also served by Silverlink as well as by the Bakerloo Line. Willesden depot (coded WN) remains although much locomotive stabling is now undertaken slightly to the north at the new sidings constructed in connection with Channel Tunnel freight services. (A123990/685957)

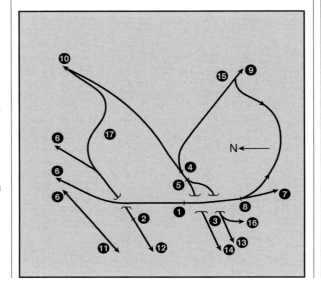

WIMBLEDON

Then: 1924
Now: 27 June 2000

As is clearly shown in the first of these photographs, Wimbledon was and is an important railway junction. Possessing 10 platform faces, at the time that the first of these two photographs was taken the local railway

network had yet to be completed — it was not until 7 July 1929 that the Wimbledon-South Merton section of the line to Sutton was opened (it was completed through to Sutton on the following 5 January) by the Southern Railway. The station illustrated in the 'Then' shot shows the station as it existed prior to the modernisation of 1929 in connection with the Portsmouth line electrification. The view shows clearly the terminal platforms used by

the District Railway — then independent but be taken over by the London Passenger Transport Board in 1933 — with the ex-LSWR main line heading towards London. The District gained access to Wimbledon by exercising running powers over the LSWR from Putney. Heading south is the ex-LBSCR/LSWR line towards Tooting. To the west of the station the LSWR main line heads towards Woking whilst the ex-LBSCR/LSWR route towards Merton Park heads southwards again. In addition to the railway interest, note also the trams and the general lack of traffic.

The first station at Wimbledon — known as Wimbledon & Merton until 1909 — was opened with the London & Southampton Railway's route from Nine Elms to Woking Common on 21 May 1838. The Wimbledon & Croydon Railway, incorporated in 1853, was opened on 22 October 1855 and was worked from the following year by the LBSCR. Authorised in 1864, the Tooting, Merton & Wimbledon Railway built a line from Streatham Junction to Wimbledon; at Tooting the line divided, with alternative routes reaching Wimbledon via Haydons Lane or via Merton Park on the line to Croydon. The TM&WR was jointly controlled by the LSWR and the LBSCR with the result that the section from Merton Park into Wimbledon passed to joint control. The line opened on

1 October 1868. District Railway trains first served Wimbledon on 3 June 1889 when the LSWR line between Wimbledon and Putney opened.

Today, Wimbledon is as important, if not more so, than it was in 1924. The scale of the station is undiminished, retaining 10 platform faces, although the station itself is not as identifiable, hidden amongst the redevelopment of the area. The goods yard, which closed in January 1970, has disappeared, being replaced by the Centre Court shopping centre. To the west of the station, an office block has been built over the track. District Line services continue to operate into the town — as evinced by the rake of stock on the station approaches from the east — whilst the majority of services through the station on the ex-LSWR main line are in the hands of South West Trains. Services operated by Thameslink and Connex South Central run into Wimbledon over the ex-TM&WR line to the east and over the Sutton lines to the west. However, whilst London's first generation trams may have disappeared, the line from Wimbledon to Croydon has now been converted for use by Croydon Tramlink; passenger services over the route were suspended from spring of 1997 until early 2000 to allow for the conversion of the route.
(10723/685960)

WOLVERHAMPTON

244

Then: 9 June 1938
Now: 25 January 2001

Viewed looking north, the close relationship between the LMS High Level — in the foreground — and GWR Low Level — in the background — stations in Wolverhampton is readily apparent in this pair of photographs. Several rakes of GWR coaching stock can be seen in Low Level and, in the far distance, is possible to see a clerestory coach. In the foreground, three LMS tank engines, including a 1930-built Fowler-designed 2-6-2T, can be seen at work.

The first railway to serve Wolverhampton was the Grand Junction Railway (later London & North Western and, by the date of the 'Then' photograph, LMS), which opened on 4 July 1837. The original GJR station serving Wolverhampton was located at Wednesfield Heath and a station on its current location was opened on 24 June 1852, when the original station was renamed Wednesfield Heath. The new station was given the suffix ' General', becoming 'Queen Street' in the following year; it was to become 'High Level' on 1 June 1885, the year after the LNWR had rebuilt it. Although predominantly LNWR, High Level also served trains over the Midland Railway route towards Walsall. The GWR's presence in the town

was partly the result of the Oxford, Worcester & Wolverhampton Railway. This standard gauge line, engineered by Brunel, was authorised in August 1845 and the section through Wolverhampton opened on 1 July 1854. Broad gauge lines reached the town via the Birmingham, Wolverhampton & Dudley Railway (another constituent of the GWR) via mixed gauge lines from Priestfield on 14 November 1854. Low Level station was designed by John Fowler and initially provided with an overall roof to the design of Brunel. Broad gauge tracks disappeared in April 1869 but the station was to undergo major rebuilding during the 1920s and 1930s. The overall roof was dismantled gradually, the work being completed by May 1934, and new platform canopies were provided; the 'Then' shot shows this work recently completed.

Although both stations remain, there has been a radical transformation over the past 60 years. High Level station remains operational but has undergone considerable transformation as a result of the electrification of the West Coast main line. Rebuilding of the station was announced in January 1962 and work commenced on 19 January 1964. The overall roof was demolished in 1965 and the original facade disappeared in January 1966. The new station was largely complete when 25kV electric services were inaugurated on 6 March 1967. Located at the east

end of the station is Wolverhampton power box, which was commissioned on 18 August 1965. Whilst Low Level station remains largely intact, it is now devoid of railway activity. To the east of the station much of the land is now occupied by a vast new Post Office sorting office, whilst much of the trackbed of the erstwhile GWR route towards Birmingham has now been resurrected to form the route of the Midland Metro. Passenger services west of Low Level station towards Stafford Road Junction were withdrawn on 4 March 1968 (with the line being lifted west of the station following this), whilst those between Low Level and Birmingham Snow Hill followed on 6 March 1972. The line between Wolverhampton Low Level and Priestfield closed completely on 23 May 1973. Access to Low Level — which had become a Parcels Concentration Depot on closure to passenger services — was now only via the ex-MR link to Heath Town Junction. The parcels depot closed officially on 1 June 1981, with the last train departing on 12 June 1981. The link to Heath Town Junction closed in October 1984. On 25 March 1986 Low Level station was officially listed as being of architectural interest; however, plans for the development of the now disused site as a transport museum seem to have come to nothing.
(57486/687626)

WORKINGTON

Then: 10 July 1958
Now: 10 January 2001

Taken looking northeastwards, this pair of photographs shows the inter-relationship between the London & North Western (in the foreground) and Cleator & Workington Junction (in the background). Dominating the foreground is the ex-LNWR Workington Main station (1) situated on the line between Whitehaven (2) and Maryport via Siddick Junction (3). Running parallel to the LNWR line is the ex-C&WJR, which ran from Siddick Junction (4), passing over the line towards Penrith (6) and through Workington Central (8) before heading south towards Distington (9). The line from Penrith headed towards the coast (5) and Workington Main station, having passed

through Workington Bridge station (7). By the date of this photograph, Workington Bridge had closed completely, all passenger and freight facilities being withdrawn on 1 January 1951. The C&WJR was also freight only by this date, passenger services having been withdrawn on 13 April 1931. There was a spur — opened on 16 March 1885 — between Workington Bridge and Cloffocks Junction, to the west of Workington Central, but this cannot be clearly identified in the photograph and was, in any case, closed on 26 March 1930.

The Cumbrian Coast route south from Maryport to Whitehaven via Workington was promoted by the Whitehaven Junction Railway, which was incorporated on 4 July 1844. The section from Maryport to Workington was opened on 19 January 1846, the line south from Workington to Harrington on 18 May 1846 and the route through to Whitehaven was opened to freight on 15 February 1847 and to passenger traffic on the following 19 March. The section of the line towards Penrith was opened under the auspices of Cockermouth & Workington Railway and opened on 28 April 1847. Both the WJR and the C&WR were to become part of the LNWR. The C&WJR was incorporated on 27 June 1876 and opened in July 1879 for freight traffic. Passenger services were introduced between Workington (Central from 1880) southwards to Moor Row on 1 October 1879 and extended to Siddick Junction on 1 September 1880. The C&WJR possessed its own locomotives, although some services were operated by the Furness and LNW railways. All lines illustrated passed to the LMS in 1923.

As elsewhere on the Cumbrian Coast — see the comparisons at Barrow and Maryport — the scene at Workington is also dramatically different. Freight facilities were withdrawn from Workington Central on 4 May 1964 and the line through the station closed completely between Harrington Junction and Calva Junction (slightly to the north of the scenes illustrated here) on 29 September 1965. The Workington-Keswick

line closed completely on 18 April 1966. Today, passenger services through Workington are provided by First North Western and there remains some freight activity. As can be seen, there has been considerable rationalisation around Workington station, although Workington Main No 3 signalbox, built by the LNWR in 1886 with a 25-lever frame, still serves the northern end of the station. In the distance, the area that once served as Workington Central has been redeveloped, although the bridge that carried the line over the River Derwent is still extant as are the embankments on either side of the river. The line of route to Keswick, however, has been largely eradicated with modern landscaping. The area occupied by the goods yard at Main still possesses track, but this appears weed-strewn and out of use.
(A72262/687531)

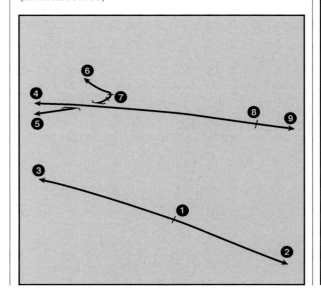

AEROFILMS

Aerofilms was founded in 1919 and has specialised in the acquisition of aerial photography within the United Kingdom throughout its history. The company has a record of being innovative in the uses and applications of aerial photography.

Photographs looking at the environment in perspective are called oblique aerial photographs. These are taken with Hasselblad cameras by professional photographers experienced in the difficult conditions encountered in aerial work.

Photographs looking straight down are termed vertical aerial photographs. These photographs are obtained using Leica survey cameras, the products from which are normally used in the making of maps.

Aerofilms has a unique library of oblique and vertical photographs in excess of one and a half million in number covering the United Kingdom. This library of photographs dates from 1919 and is being continually updated.

Oblique and vertical photography can be taken to customers' specification by Aerofilms' professional photographers.

To discover more of the wealth of past or present photographs held in the library at Aerofilms or to commission new aerial photographs, please contact:

Aerofilms Ltd
Gate Studios
Station Road
Borehamwood
Herts
WD6 1EJ

Telephone: 020 8207 0666
Fax: 020 8207 5433